Tanya Marlow

# TREASURES IN Straw

Exploring the griefs and gifts of the Christmas story

BRF
Ministries

BRF Ministries
15 The Chambers, Vineyard
Abingdon OX14 3FE
**+44(0)1865 319700 | brf.org.uk**

Bible Reading Fellowship (BRF) is a charity (233280) and company limited by guarantee (301324), registered in England and Wales

EU Authorised Representative: Easy Access System Europe – Mustamäe tee 50, 10621 Tallinn, Estonia, **gpsr.requests@easproject.com**

ISBN 978 1 80039 567 1
First published 2026
10 9 8 7 6 5 4 3 2 1 0


Cover illustrated by Rose Edwards



A catalogue record for this book is available from the British Library.

Printed and bound by CPI Group (UK) Ltd, Croydon CR0 4YY

‘Finally, an Advent book for all of us – for those who weep and mourn as much as for those who anticipate and celebrate. Release your pent-up breath and receive God’s loving balm as you read this treasure.’
**Amy Boucher Pye, author of *Celebrating Christmas***

‘Tanya Marlow has written a rare and beautiful book. With theological depth, pastoral wisdom, and remarkable emotional intelligence, Marlow re-enters the Christmas story not through nostalgia, but through the lived realities of ordinary people carrying hidden wounds. She reveals how the incarnation speaks not only to joy, but also to infertility, chronic illness, loneliness, trauma, exclusion, war, poverty, and fear. The result is a devotional work that feels both deeply contemporary and timelessly Christian. This is theology at its most pastoral and pastoral care at its most theological.’
**Revd Dr Timothy Goode, Canon for Congregational Discipleship and Nurture at York Minster, and author of *Breaking, Not Broken***

‘As a reader, I look forward to returning to this book each Advent, and as a speaker, I look forward to pointing others to the wisdom in its pages.’
**Naomi Hutchison, poet and speaker**

‘This book is written with warmth, wit, and courage, and refuses to settle for a one-dimensional view of the festive season. A moving, accessible, and soul-soothing read. This is the Christmas devotional that was waiting to be written.’
**Revd Dr Trystan Owain Hughes, author of *Living the Prayer* and *To Hell’s Mouth and Back***

‘What a gift this book is. Tanya has unearthed riches for us to treasure amid the realities of everyday life. I highly recommend pondering each passage and lingering longer over the reflection that follows.’
**Cathy Madavan, author, speaker, and coach**

‘*Treasures in Straw* is a kind and wise friend to remind us of the treasure of Jesus’ coming amidst the darkness we face in the world.’
**Rachael Newham, theologian and author**

‘A truly stunning and thought-provoking read which brings alive the old, old stories of Christmas. If you have ever searched for meaning behind the tinsel and treats of this season, then I urge you to take up Tanya’s invitation to join her on a revealing journey which looks unflinchingly at the human realities of the nativity both then and now.’
**Revd Dr Emma Pennington, Canon Missioner, Canterbury Cathedral, and author of *All Shall Be Well***

‘Refusing to sentimentalise the nativity story, Tanya Marlow offers us something hopeful and authentic: a vision of God with us in the midst of our real human pain and struggle. I have huge respect for Tanya as a thinker, communicator, and activist. She embodies the hope she describes, making this the perfect way to enter the Advent season.’
**Revd Will Van Der Hart, priest and author**

‘Tanya brings the grit back into this sanitised season while always pointing us to hope. You’ll see Christmas’ characters caked with the same dust your own life carries, then discover the promises given to them are the same promises given to you. This is the kind of devotional writing I need. Show me Christmas’ griefs so my own are given context. Show me its gifts so I might enter its joys. Show me the manger and a God clothed in flesh. *Treasures in Straw* does all this and more.’
**Sheridan Voysey, author of *Resurrection Year* and *The Making of Us***

‘I read this book with a deep appreciation of its authenticity and encouragement. Tanya Marlow writes open-eyed about the realities of God’s people’s life experiences, their highs and lows, then and now. A genuinely valuable devotional book for Advent and Christmas-tide.’
**Revd Dr Jenni Williams, vicar of St Matthew’s with St Luke’s Oxford**

‘I love Marlow’s thoughtful reading of the Christmas narrative and her insights born from personal experience, the historical and biblical work of scholars, African theologians, and much more. *Treasures in Straw* is a beautiful book to read and share with others.’
**April Yamasaki, pastor and author of *Sacred Pauses*, *Four Gifts*, and *Hope Beyond Our Sorrows***

*For my parents,*
*who love Jesus exuberantly*
*and were the first to teach me that faith can be an adventure.*

# Contents

# Introduction

How do you feel about Christmas? Generally, I love it. For me, Christmas means comforting traditions, little treats and inspirations throughout Advent, and the delight of watching my son opening his presents – spiritual, emotional, and physical nourishment.

For my friend Helen Austin, it is quite different. Issues with grief, mental illness, and chronic physical illness (including having a restricted diet) have made it harder to enjoy the day itself. Being single at Christmas-tide, when everyone is talking about their fun family gatherings, plus being childless (not by choice) at a festival focused on childbirth cruelly accentuates the losses Helen feels in everyday life. In December 2025, Helen confessed on Facebook that for several years she 'avoided all things Christmas, including church, for the whole month of December, because it was just all so painful'. She is not alone in this.

## Emotions and the Christmas phenomenon

Christmas is a megaphone. In the west, particularly the UK, we have established Christmas as the magical bringer of joy, cosiness, and warmth in winter, quality time with a loving family, perfect presents, good food, and, perhaps above all, children filled with wonder. Neuroscience tells us that if we grew up enjoying Christmas, then every ritual and tradition associated with Christmas will reinforce our 'classic conditioning' to automatically feel positive with each reminder. Like Pavlov's dog salivating every time a bell rings, we experience that Christmassy glow every time we put up decorations, sing carols, or, ironically enough, hear bells ringing. If we are happy in life, Christmas-tide has the power to amplify that feeling.

Unfortunately, joy is not the only feeling Christmas can intensify. Because there is so much expectation of Christmassy perfection built upon this one day of the year, if our circumstances prevent us from having a happy Christmas, the grief is so much stronger on this day. Nothing bad is supposed to happen on birthdays, holidays, or Christmas Day, so if it does the sense of betrayal is even more pronounced. Every Christmassy ritual then becomes a mocking reminder of all that is lost.

Kenneth Doka called this experience 'disenfranchised grief': grief not validated by society.[1] It is frowned upon to *express* sadness or look for support from others at a time of communal feasting. People will sympathise with you losing your job, but not if you want to process it at a child's birthday dinner. Society expects us to feel happy at weddings and sad at funerals. It's only polite. Thanks to Charles Dickens' *A Christmas Carol*, we even have an insult for someone who doesn't feel happy at Christmastime – a Scrooge. If you express the wrong emotion, society will punish you for it.

Disenfranchised grief can also include *feeling* sad. Arlie Hochschild observed that emotions are not just personal and isolated, but heavily influenced by cultural expectations, which she calls 'feeling rules'.[2] That pressure is so strong that if we aren't experiencing the expected communal reaction naturally, we do what Hochschild calls 'emotion work'. This involves not only concealing our feelings in front of others, so we don't display the 'wrong' emotion in our faces, but also trying to control the emotion itself. The only single person in a roomful of happy couples stifles the feeling of loneliness and tells himself he really is having fun. The teen who asked for an Xbox and got a board game instead desperately tries to quash their disappointment and summon up gratitude. The recently bereaved grandmother spends Christmas Day smiling for the sake of the kids, while trying to numb the chasm of grief.

Then, if we are Christians, we add the extra expectation of being obliged to rejoice at Christmas because Jesus was born. The cultural obligation of feeling happy now extends to sacred spaces and religious communities, where we really *ought* to be happy – because 'Jesus'. Our emotions become a measure of our devotion. Yet even if we do feel happy, our motivation must be scrutinised. I remember feeling guilty as a child because I knew I should feel most happy about Jesus being born for us, but I was honestly more excited about getting roller skates.

It is exhausting, and it is no wonder that so many people avoid Christmas altogether. The jarring juxtaposition of the world's merriment and our pain is just too much to bear.

## Christmas versus nativity

The reason I wrote this book was because I saw such a difference between Christmas as we mark it today versus the original story of the nativity. Then, there was joy, yes, and gifts, but there was also sorrow and sacrifice. Mary had a baby, the saviour of the whole world, but not everyone was happy about it, most notably Herod. The images on Christmas cards are of holy mother, father, baby, all perfect and respectable, but the nativity had a non-typical family structure, with Joseph as stepfather and Mary probably suspected of sexual impropriety.

Christmas today is obsessed with children's happiness, though this wasn't always the case. For centuries in Britain, Christmas was a lengthy, communal, mainly adult festival for several days, intended for resting after the harvesting (with rowdy and alcoholic revelry). The Victorians, desiring societal control, shifted Christmas to one day only: nuclear families with their well-behaved, innocent children, quietly, privately, celebrating around their fir trees at home. Then it was back to the factory the next day. Materialism and greed then spawned the modern, jolly, gift-giving, cola-bringing Santa in the 20th century.

Yet the good news of Christ was not aimed at individuals or even families but marginalised communities and forgotten peoples. The 'perfect' Christmas today is easier to achieve if you're rich; yet Christ was born into poverty, and Mary sang triumphantly about the rich being sent away.

As I looked again through the original Christmas story, I saw that loss and sacrifice were everywhere. Against that dark backdrop, the gift of God-with-us shone more brightly. The losses within the nativity were temporal, relational, or material, but the gains were spiritual and eternal. It was less about cosy stables and more about upending unjust societies. It was less about individual gifts and more about communal equality.

The costs were often great, but the reward of Jesus was greater. The griefs were deep, but the joys lasted longer. They had a taste of God's kingdom in Christ's first coming, and the promise of fulfilment in Christ's second coming.

They and then is also us and now. Life is good and glorious but also hard and painful. We celebrate and rejoice that Jesus came, and we also long for Jesus' coming. We love our world but also grieve for it and crave its restoration. We are thankful for our personal blessings and torn apart by our personal sufferings.

## How to read this book

This book is designed to be a journey from 1 December to 6 January, from Advent to Epiphany, in six sections. We start with older prophecies, walk through the Christmas story in roughly chronological order, then begin the new year with themes of loss and gain in Paul's writings.

- **Kingdom reversals** asks what are God's promises to people who live without hope?
- **Honour and favour** digs into Jesus' cultural context. How does God restore people shamed by society?
- **Songs after silence** considers silence and waiting as preparation for God's gifts, and asks is it possible to sing songs of joy after disaster has come?
- **Giving up** looks at sacrifice and surrender. When should we give things up, give things away, or give our worries upwards (to God)?

- **Pierced hearts** comes after Christmas, exploring grief and trauma. How can the wisdom, lament, and empathy in the Christmas stories help us heal?
- **Living as losers** looks forward to the new year and to our ultimate future. When we add up the costs and rewards of the Christian life, is it all worth it?

Each devotion includes a reading from the NIV, a reflection, questions to consider, and a chance to spend time in prayer. Running throughout, I have included inspiring stories of Christians today who have lived through these issues, just like the original Bible characters.

Christmas devotionals are notorious for being abandoned halfway through as the season gets busier, so do give yourself permission to start early or catch up and speed-read when you've missed a few days. Or wait for a quieter moment and read it in weekly sections rather than day by day. The book has a flow, arc, and transformational purpose, and the full journey is worth undertaking, I promise.

## Grief and gift

Nowadays Christmas feels like either grief or gift; the nativity is both grief and gift together.

God has entered our world and experienced it fully, the good and the bad. At his second coming, Jesus will entirely restore the world. One day, it will be all gift; until then, we live with both.

Christmas can sometimes feel superficial or smug, but the nativity was not saccharine, tinselled jollity, isolated from the world's problems. The nativity was mess and order, peace and disruption, joy and sorrow, darkness and light, disgrace and honour, danger and protection, poverty and provision, uncertainty and hope, temptation and tyranny, grief and celebration. All of life is there, raw and true. And all are invited in.

My invitation to you this season is to look afresh at the original Christmas story, with the freedom to be honest in lament, exuberant in praise, or both together. Whether you love Christmas or dread it, this is a chance to treasure those forgotten spiritual blessings that do not perish or fade, and rediscover genuine delight in Jesus, our greatest gift.

1

# Kingdom reversals

## 1 December

# Those in darkness are given light

**Tiglath-Pileser king of Assyria came and took… Gilead and Galilee, including all the land of Naphtali, and deported the people to Assyria.**
2 KINGS 15:29

**Nevertheless, there will be no more gloom for those who were in distress. In the past he humbled the land of Zebulun and the land of Naphtali, but in the future he will honour Galilee of the nations, by the Way of the Sea, beyond the Jordan –**
**The people walking in darkness**
**have seen a great light;**
**on those living in the land of deep darkness**
**a light has dawned.**
ISAIAH 9:1–2

Lucy remembers December 2022 as the year the lights went out. Too unwell to work, surviving on benefits alone, she was alarmed to see there was an erroneous charge on her gas and electric account. When she rang, the power company acknowledged the mistake, but it would take time to fix. Lucy kept feeding the meter at home, but a glitch meant she was only getting pennies' worth from £10.

She ran out of money (and therefore power) just as temperatures plummeted. When she rang customer service, a snowstorm disrupted their phone lines. When she rang the council, they promised to investigate, but her phone ran out of charge, and they never visited. She refused friends' offers of a loan, fearing she couldn't repay them. In the dark and cold, she became ill.

Finally, mini-miracles occurred, in the shape of human kindness. A neighbour kept her stocked in hot-water bottles and charged her phone. A mystery giver put an envelope of cash through her door. A sympathetic power company employee gave her a code to add £100 to her account. Lucy trudged through the snow, still unwell, for two days, looking for a post office willing to give her an electric card for free so she could add the code. Finally, one did. And there was light.

'That was the year I believed the Christmas story could possibly be real,' Lucy said. As an atheist, she still wasn't convinced of God's existence, but now she could just about believe there once was an innkeeper generous enough to offer help to people in need. 'My Christmas was saved by people giving what they could and not expecting anything back. The anonymous gift made me able, emotionally, to claim the help I needed and not feel guilty about it. It made me believe that it's not just me: other people will go out of their way to help too.'

Lucy's story moves me for many reasons: the precariousness of poverty; how unreliable society's safety nets are; how hard it is to ask for help when you have little to give back; how anonymous cash handouts without strings attached are often exactly what is needed – but most of all, how the kindness of strangers had seemed as much a fairytale to her as God being born on earth. When you have lived in darkness, literally and metaphorically, it takes its toll.

Isaiah's original audience had plenty of reasons for 'distress' and 'gloom' (Isaiah 9:1). In c. 733BC, Galilee was the first area to be razed to the ground by the notorious Assyrian king Tiglath-Pileser III (2 Kings 15:29).

Galilee was ruined and never really recovered. Meanwhile, the regions lucky enough to survive Assyria's assaults, like Jerusalem, grew proud.

Even in Jesus' day, hundreds of years later, the Jerusalemites looked down on the Galileans.

The Galileans were a devastated people struggling to survive. Through Isaiah, God speaks to a 'humbled' people and promises to 'honour' them (Isaiah 9:1). At their lowest point, God doesn't forget them. There is hope. Although they are in darkness now, light will come, and it will be a 'great light' (Isaiah 9:2). There is hope for us, too. Darkness is not only a place of terror; it can also be the warm womb where the Spirit of God broods. Darkness can be the nurturing precursor to new life.

God has a habit of doing this. Back in Genesis, all was dark, yet 'the Spirit of God was hovering over the waters' (Genesis 1:2–3), and God spoke light into the world. When the Israelites wandered in the desert, they were led by a pillar of fire by night to show that God was with them (Exodus 13:21). The psalmist called God's law 'a light on my path' (Psalm 119:105), and when David was protected from Saul's attacks, he declared: 'My God turns my darkness into light' (Psalm 18:28).

Light therefore signifies creation, new life, hope, and God's presence, protection, and guidance. Then Jesus comes and declares that he is all of these: 'I am the light of the world. Whoever follows me will never walk in darkness' (John 8:12).

The 'people walking in darkness' become those who 'will never walk in darkness'. Jesus is good news for forgotten peoples, dismissed minority groups, and those in pain whose cries are ignored. If you feel surrounded by darkness right now, remember our future – an eternity when 'there will be no night' (Revelation 21:25). Meanwhile, in our current dark places, Jesus is our light, and his presence is our hope, however dim it may seem sometimes.

On a dark December day, I light a candle.

## Reflect

- What areas of your life feel dark and in need of God's light?
- What areas of the world seem gloomy and despairing? How might you pray for them?

Take time to listen to 'The people that walked in darkness' from Handel's *Messiah* and use it as a prayer.

## Pray

*In the midst of despair, may I know your hope.*
*In the midst of gloom, may I feel your presence.*
*In the midst of darkness, may I walk in your light. Amen.*

## 2 December

# The battle-weary are given peace

**You have enlarged the nation**
**and increased their joy;**
**they rejoice before you**
**as people rejoice at the harvest,**
**as warriors rejoice**
**when dividing the plunder.**
**For as in the day of Midian's defeat,**
**you have shattered**
**the yoke that burdens them,**
**the bar across their shoulders,**
**the rod of their oppressor.**
**Every warrior's boot used in battle**
**and every garment rolled in blood**
**will be destined for burning,**
**will be fuel for the fire.**

ISAIAH 9:3–5

Stas is a minister of a church in Lviv, Ukraine, but from 2022 to 2024 he was also serving in the military, fighting Russia's invasion. 'I can't completely express what I faced,' he confessed. One story he did share was watching another soldier spray-wash the inside of a van that had been used for transporting dead bodies. He opened the van door and out poured a sticky slew of blood and entrails.

'This can break you,' Stas confessed. He is grateful for the support of fellow Christians who carried him through.[3]

We often think of peace in Christian circles as a *feeling* we experience individually, but in Isaiah, peace primarily means an end to war. Isaiah's prophecy of hope to Galilee continues with a blessing for 'the nation'(v. 3), then hints at something larger still: global peace.

Isaiah prophetically imagines a day of unexpected victory, where the underdogs win against the giant, 'as in the day of Midian's defeat' (v. 4). Centuries before Isaiah's day, God gave Gideon victory over thousands of Midianites with just 300 men (Judges 7). This showed it was God's salvation, not military power, that won the day. In Isaiah, God is reminding Galilee that however big our oppressor, God can defeat them. Today, even as we feel powerless to stop wars, we know that God can still intervene against all odds, and our prayers are valuable.

God promises to shatter 'the yoke that burdens them', rescuing the vulnerable, and break 'the rod of their oppressor', putting an end to dictators' power (v. 4). There is more than this, however. It's not just that God will one day win the battle, it's that the time for war itself will be ended, 'Every warrior's boot used in battle... will be destined for burning' (v. 5).

The king who will come, as Isaiah goes on to say, will be called the 'Prince of Peace' (Isaiah 9:6). African theologian Alfred Sebahene points out that peace is a communal concept, not merely a personal state: 'There will be no peace if it is only experienced by the individual.'[4]

Jesus came to end human fighting and bring peace between God and humanity. In World War II, there were two key moments of victory. The first was D-Day, when the world knew who would win; the second was VE Day, when Hitler was finally defeated and people throughout Europe celebrated on the streets that war was over. Jesus' first coming, at Christmas, is D-Day, the declaration of peace; his second coming, at the end of time, is VE Day, the end to all war. When Jesus' peace comes, joy follows.

If you are feeling battle-weary, literally or metaphorically, perhaps you can take comfort in knowing our certain future. Evil will not win the day. Peace will come. Joy will follow. In between, we wait in hope.

## Reflect

- What do you think about the concept of peace not being individually experienced but communal?
- Which areas of the world or people known to you need your prayers for peace?
- How does the image of D-Day versus VE Day help you?
- Take time to listen to 'Rejoice greatly' from Handel's *Messiah* and use it as a prayer.

## Pray

*Dear Lord, thank you for always being on the side of the oppressed, not the oppressor. Please minister to all those suffering from warfare today. I long for an end to war and pray for your peace in this world. Amen.*

## 3 December

# The hard-pressed are given relief

**For to us a child is born,**
**to us a son is given,**
**and the government will be on his shoulders.**
**And he will be called**
**Wonderful Counsellor, Mighty God,**
**Everlasting Father, Prince of Peace.**
**Of the greatness of his government and peace**
**there will be no end.**
**He will reign on David's throne**
**and over his kingdom,**
**establishing and upholding it**
**with justice and righteousness**
**from that time on and forever.**
**The zeal of the Lord Almighty**
**will accomplish this.**
ISAIAH 9:6–7

**'Come to me, all you who are weary and burdened, and I will give you rest. Take my yoke upon you and learn from me, for I am gentle and humble in heart, and you will find rest for your souls. For my yoke is easy and my burden is light.'**
MATTHEW 11:28–30

When I was 20, I travelled to southern Africa with a Christian organisation. All my belongings for a month were tightly packed in a long, thin rucksack which, because I'm only 5'4", started at my hips and ended at the top of my head. Trudging from the bus to our accommodation, I grew accustomed to the weight on my shoulders, only occasionally aware of the pain. But when we arrived and I could swing the bag off and on to the floor, my whole body felt like it was floating. The relief was overwhelming.

That, I imagine, is how it feels to be released from a yoke. Typically, a yoke is a wooden bar fixed over the necks of a pair of oxen and attached to a plough or wagon behind them so they can pull it together. In the Bible, it is an image often signifying oppression or captivity, as indeed Isaiah alluded to: 'the yoke that burdens them, the bar across their shoulders' (Isaiah 9:4). Corrupt leaders benefit themselves by burdening their people, and the population carries the weight of their selfish rule.

Here, however, Isaiah promises that not only will peace to end all war emerge from Galilee but also a king to top all kings. This future leader ticks all the boxes: a descendant of the great King David; a judge who upholds righteousness and justice; a wise sage who gives wonderful advice; and a prince who brings peace and wholeness. He will take all the weight and pressure of ruling upon himself: 'the government will be on his shoulders' (v. 6).

Yet there is still more. Although he is described as a 'child [who] is born' (v. 6), this is no ordinary human leader. He is given titles that belong to God the creator alone, 'Mighty God, Everlasting Father', and he will rule forever (vv. 6–7). The only one to fit this description is Jesus. The Mighty God becomes a vulnerable infant.

When Jesus arrives, he also mentions a yoke. Rather than us carrying our hardships alone, he invites us to be joined to him so he can take the lead. His strength will pull the load for us.

We see again the two horizons of Christ's rule: now and not yet. One day all tyrants and petty bullies will be judged definitively, and Jesus' reign of peace will be established.

Even today, as we are weighed down and threatened by dictators large and small, we can shift our eyes to Jesus, whose power and gentleness is exponentially greater. We live under the yoke of bad human rulers, but Jesus' spiritual kingdom runs in parallel, bringing hope and help.

Jesus shifts heavy burdens off our shoulders, on to his. Though our situation may remain unchanged, most things are slightly more bearable after prayer. Jesus' invitation to us is to walk alongside him: his yoke is easy; his burden is light.

## Reflect

- As you consider the oppressors in your life, what difference does it make to see Christ's reign as the greater spiritual reality?
- What burdens do you need to ask Jesus to lift today?
- Which oppressed peoples can you bring to God today?

Take time to listen to 'Rejoice greatly' and 'He shall feed his flock' from Handel's *Messiah* and use them as prayers for yourself and the world.

## Pray

As you listen, experiment with rolling your shoulders up and back, feeling the tension release, and ask Jesus to lift your burdens too.

# 4 December

## The little will become great

**'But you, Bethlehem Ephrathah,**
**though you are small among the clans of Judah,**
**out of you will come for me**
**one who will be ruler over Israel,**
**whose origins are from of old,**
**from ancient times.'**
**Therefore Israel will be abandoned**
**until the time when she who is in labour bears a son,**
**and the rest of his brothers return**
**to join the Israelites.**
**He will stand and shepherd his flock**
**in the strength of the Lord,**
**in the majesty of the name of the Lord his God.**
**And they will live securely, for then his greatness**
**will reach to the ends of the earth.**
**And he will be our peace**
**when the Assyrians invade our land**
**and march through our fortresses.**

MICAH 5:2–5A

For 14 years I lived in Plymouth, a large seaside city in the southwest of England. I loved it, so it puzzled me how so many others, particularly from the southeast, disparaged the town. Even the locals would make self-deprecating jokes about being a 'Janner'. Plymouth is steeped in history, with blue plaques commemorating all who set sail from its harbour: Sir Francis Drake, Captain Cook, Charles Darwin, and the

Mayflower pilgrims. But visitors quip that Plymouth is only known for people leaving it.

I imagine this is how Bethlehem felt at the time the prophet Micah was writing. In a sense, it is strange that the people of Bethlehem should feel insignificant. After all, they already had the historical honour of living in the birthplace of David, the greatest king thus far. Yet now, their glory faded, they were only aware of their smallness, so Micah offered them encouragement.

Some context is needed here. This chapter likely envisages the moment when the Assyrian king, Sennacherib, besieged Jerusalem in 701BC, which was approximately 30 years after the Assyrians attacked Galilee. The siege (and God's miraculous rescue) is described in 2 Kings 18—19. 'When the Assyrians invade our land and march through our fortresses,' Micah promises, 'He will be our peace' (v. 5). But who is 'he'?

Like Isaiah, Micah saw beyond the current crisis to a future king. Micah 4 describes God's people as 'Daughter Zion', who were suffering in labour during the exile but would later be rescued (Micah 4:8–10). Micah 5 then foretells a time when 'she who is in labour bears a son' (5:3). This 'son' would rule 'to the ends of the earth' (v. 4). Like King David, he would come from Bethlehem (v. 2) and would 'shepherd his flock' (v. 4).

If we recall, Isaiah 9 had prophesied that the Prince of Peace, a great light, would break the darkness of Galilee. Micah 5, however, promised that the Messiah would arise from Bethlehem. Israel's scholars must have puzzled over how this ruler was linked to both Galilee and Bethlehem, two overlooked towns at opposite ends of the land. That is, until Jesus was born to Mary, whose hometown was Nazareth in Galilee, and Joseph, whose family originated from Bethlehem. It is a reminder that God has the power to solve the unsolvable and reveal, in time, there was a plan all along.

Micah's message now rings out through the ages for those individuals or communities who feel puny, little, or insignificant. It is a word of truth for anyone who feels like their glory days are behind them. Bethlehem thought that the greatest blue plaque for their town would be the birth of David. Then the creator and saviour of the universe was born there, and that former accolade paled into insignificance. The best was yet to come.

Because of the Holy Spirit, our very bodies have the greatest honour of all: God is in residence there. Jesus' blue plaque is marked on our hearts, and heaven is our future home. When we feel insignificant and overlooked, God says, 'I haven't forgotten you.' When we feel like our glory days are long gone, God whispers this spiritual truth, 'The best is yet to come.'

## Reflect

- What does it mean to you to remember 'the best is yet to come'?
- Which people or communities may need reminding that God loves the underdogs?

Take time to listen to 'Because of Bethlehem' by Matthew West.

## Review

- In this section, how have God's kingdom reversals comforted you? How have they challenged you?

## Pray

*Dear Lord, on the days where I feel puny and insignificant, remind me that Jesus dwells in me, with a blue plaque upon my heart. On the days where I feel the best is behind me, remind me of my glorious future. Amen.*

2

# Honour and favour

# Introduction

Inger's worst Christmas was during Covid lockdown in 2021. The day had begun with several hours in hospital with her learning-disabled son, as his symptoms looked like sepsis. Though he was cleared and sent home, he then developed gastro-enteritis, and because of his disability he had no control over his bowels.

And so it was that Inger was literally washing faeces out of soiled clothes when her husband hovered with a strange, excited agitation and gave her the worst news of her life in a succession of emotional blows.

'I just have to tell you something. I'd grown tired of online porn; it just wasn't doing it for me anymore.'

*BAM.*

'So, I turned to websites where I've been paying women for online sex.'

*BAM.*

'And I've become totally obsessed with this one woman. She's so beautiful. I just have to have sex with her.'

*BAM.*

'So, I'm going to fly out to Colombia to be with her. You can't expect me to live without her; she's my only chance at happiness.'

*BAM. BAM. BAM.*

He was an ordained minister, and they had been married for 27 years. Although Inger had suspected that something was troubling her husband, she thought it was an issue they would deal with together, as partners. Nothing prepared her for the shock that he was abandoning their marriage for a sex worker. At that moment, reeling from these revelations, she felt as though she were floating above reality, yet her hands kept washing the filth out of the dirty clothes.

In the aftermath, as her husband ultimately resigned as a church minister and flew to South America, she realised that it was not just her marriage and an active co-parent she was losing. She also lost her identity and status as a minister's wife, which had been important to her. Her husband's actions caused not only private heartbreak but also changed how others saw her.

## Honour and shame

Inger's story illustrates something about the nature of honour and shame, important concepts in Jesus' day. In contrast to our modern, individualised western societies, the first-century Mediterranean cultures were group-centred and 'collectivist' societies. It wasn't about cultivating self-esteem (how you value yourself), but cultivating honour, which was about how your tribe and wider society assessed your worth. Whereas we ask, 'Who am I?', they would define themselves by asking, 'Who do people say I am?' (Mark 8:27).[5]

Individual honest expression was less important than conforming to the expectations of the family, ancestors, and tribe. You did not just represent yourself but something much wider, and your first responsibility was therefore to them, not yourself. Today's honour–shame cultures can be found in Asia, South America, Africa, and in Arabic countries, so as we study the familiar story, it can be helpful to think of Jesus being born in one of these contexts, rather than a western one.

How does shame feel? Shame is self-disgust or revulsion from being exposed negatively in some sort of public way. While guilt springs from our own wrong actions, shame is not necessarily connected with our own sin. A child who survives abuse can feel inner revulsion, but that shame is caused by others' wrongdoing, not theirs. Indeed, shame is often not connected to any actions or logic at all. In some cultures, having darker skin is viewed as shameful; in others, it is poverty or disability that stigmatises you. Shame is the cloud that society arbitrarily blows on to us, following us around and clinging to our skin.

In our culture, being shamed in front of the group is devastating enough (for example, the whole class laughing at the kid who wet their pants). In an honour–shame collectivistic culture, it is even worse and can have lasting consequences.

If an individual is honoured, the group also increases its worth. If the individual is shamed, that too reflects on the group. If the shame is particularly severe, the individual risks expulsion from the group or even death.

## The paradoxes of shame and glory

As you read through the nativity story, I invite you to view it through the lenses of honour and shame. Infertility is still often held as a painful secret by couples today; in Jesus' day this would have been a public, much-discussed shame. For those of us who have experienced public humiliation or false accusation, we can take to heart the stories of Elizabeth, Mary, and Joseph. In the eyes of the crowd, they lose their worth, yet in the eyes of God, they are honoured and exalted.

Jesus is the perfect example of this paradox of shame and honour. On the cross, he died the most humiliating death, naked and weak. Jesus experienced the awfulness of being publicly dishonoured. Crucifixion was a method of execution designed to shame the victim; yet we know that in God's eyes, the cross is the ultimate moment of glory.

When we think of the gifts that Jesus' incarnation brings, honour in the place of shame is rarely mentioned, yet it is one of Luke's main focuses. These issues are rarely thought about in western society or talked about in western churches, yet so many silently struggle with feeling like a failure or reject, unworthy of honour by God or others. By focusing on God's verdict instead of our 'tribe', we can shake off society's shaming and hold our heads high.

## Life after dishonour

A few years after that awful Christmas, I asked Inger about whether she felt shamed because of her ex-husband's actions.

'No,' she replied firmly. 'The shame belongs with him, not with me.' She paused, then added, 'And God honoured me. In prayer, I heard God saying to me, "You are special and beautiful, and this does not diminish you." I have held on to that.'

Inger lost her marriage. But she can testify already to the gifts that came from that devastating Christmas Day. In retrospect, she realised that her husband was emotionally abusive, making her feel small. Her life is now filled with positivity and freedom, and she goes on adventures with her son that they wouldn't have done otherwise. Wonderfully, she also has a church family which has embraced her, loved her, and respected her. There is life after dishonour.

I am disabled, and I live in a society that sees disabled partners, parents and employees as less valuable than their abled counterparts. To most, I am viewed as worth less; to a few, I am seen as worthless. For individuals and communities shamed by society, family, or the church, it can feel like an exhausting battle to value ourselves. The challenge of this next section of devotions is to change our perspective. While the world may rage or our minds may shout that we're worthless, disgusting, or despised, the nativity story quietly invites us to see ourselves through God's eyes: honoured, favoured, dearly loved. It may still be a battle, but God is firmly on our side.

# 5 December

## Losing a dream

**In the time of Herod king of Judea there was a priest named Zechariah, who belonged to the priestly division of Abijah; his wife Elizabeth was also a descendant of Aaron. Both of them were righteous in the sight of God, observing all the Lord's commands and decrees blamelessly. But they were childless because Elizabeth was not able to conceive, and they were both very old.**

LUKE 1:5–7

The Christmas story is so focused on pregnancy and miracle births that even hearing the familiar Bible passages read can be brutal for anyone who longs for a child but cannot have one. This is why I wanted to pause here, at the beginning of Zechariah and Elizabeth's story, which mentions their long experience of infertility. Although their story ends with the birth of John the Baptist, there are so many more of us who do not have their heart's desire fulfilled in this way. How can you live a life of faith knowing that God has kept you from your dream?

Sheridan and Merryn Voysey wrestled with this as a childless couple.[6] They underwent ten wilderness years, living in the limbo of trying for a baby but seeing no results. Medical routes, fostering, and adoption all came to nothing. Then, finally, after a round of IVF, Merryn had a positive pregnancy test. They were overjoyed.

It was Christmas Eve when the clinic phoned and broke the devastating news: the test had been a false positive. There was no baby. At Christmas time, the promise of this long-awaited gift was snatched away. It felt cruel.

In the decade of trying for a child, Sheridan experienced a whole range of emotions: grief; anger at the unfairness; exhausting, continual disappointment; helplessness; and even a sense of spiritual failure.

That last feeling, spiritual failure, is common to many of us who have had prayers unanswered, though few talk about it. The shadowy falsehood creeps in – that God is punishing us for unknown sin.

On this point, there is some comfort to be found in today's passage. Zechariah and Elizabeth were the perfect godly couple. Zechariah was a priest, a holy calling, and he had an impressive ancestry. Elizabeth, too, came from Aaron's priestly line. As far as spiritual credentials went, they had them in spades.

Of course, God is more concerned with someone's character, so how did they hold up on this front? In Jesus' time, many would have understood infertility to be a judgement from God, so Luke goes out of his way to emphasise both their righteousness and their obedience, 'observing *all* the Lord's decrees and commands *blamelessly*' (Luke 1:6, italics added).

Yet they were childless. In first-century Israel, Elizabeth would have been blamed for her 'barrenness' and shamed by society, the centre of others' gossip. Friends would have suggested that Zechariah divorce Elizabeth, as he was legally entitled to do. Shockingly, friends of infertile couples still whisper this suggestion today. Zechariah's righteousness is shown, in part, by his loyalty to her. Even though they eventually became parents, as Abraham and Sarah did, there is still a great deal of mystery in why God allowed them all so many years of exhausting disappointment.

Although Sheridan and Merryn's journey did not end in parenthood, they can point to other, unexpected gifts. After they closed the door on their dream, they discovered new adventures. Though it took time, Merryn can now say truthfully, 'I feel very blessed.'

Additionally, Sheridan can see in retrospect that the experience helped them grow in their faith. 'Mature faith is not necessarily that we come out more triumphant or more victorious at the end,' he explained. 'I actually think it's that we live with a lot more tension… but we still hold on to a God who's… bigger than us.'[7]

The grief of infertility can be overwhelming, and even good alternative opportunities cannot erase that. All too often, grief and gift are intertwined. In our disappointments, however, we can try to remember that God is not punishing us or being cruel and that we are not failures. Acknowledging the pain and mystery of broken dreams, we cling to the God who is bigger than us.

## Reflect

- What do you think being 'righteous' looks like today?
- What helps you cling to God when the door closes on longed-for dreams?

## Pray

*Dear Lord,*
*in our disappointments and broken dreams,*
*walk beside us, we pray.*
*Please protect our hearts,*
*reassure us of your love,*
*and lift our eyes to the possibility of unexpected gifts*
*in the here and now.*
*Amen.*

# 6 December

## Zechariah gains a son

**Once when Zechariah's division was on duty and he was serving as priest before God, he was chosen by lot, according to the custom of the priesthood, to go into the temple of the Lord and burn incense. And when the time for the burning of incense came, all the assembled worshippers were praying outside.**

**Then an angel of the Lord appeared to him, standing at the right side of the altar of incense. When Zechariah saw him, he was startled and was gripped with fear. But the angel said to him: 'Do not be afraid, Zechariah; your prayer has been heard. Your wife Elizabeth will bear you a son, and you are to call him John. He will be a joy and delight to you, and many will rejoice because of his birth, for he will be great in the sight of the Lord. He is never to take wine or other fermented drink, and he will be filled with the Holy Spirit even before he is born. He will bring back many of the people of Israel to the Lord their God. And he will go on before the Lord, in the spirit and power of Elijah, to turn the hearts of the parents to their children and the disobedient to the wisdom of the righteous – to make ready a people prepared for the Lord.'**

LUKE 1:8–17

An apocryphal story tells of a radio host in Washington D.C. who asked several ambassadors what they most wanted for Christmas. 'I wish for world peace,' the Polish ambassador said. 'An end to hunger,' said the Zambian ambassador, and the Brazilian ambassador, 'Justice for all.'

'And when we asked what the British ambassador wanted for Christmas,' the radio host announced, 'he said, "A large box of candied fruit, please."'

Most of us, deep down, long for the world to be a better place. But if I'm honest and free in my prayer times, I spend less time pleading for the end of war and more time on 'candied fruit'. Though I only rarely pray for a lottery win, I do pray for help in my writing, modest success, sunshine for our holiday. I also continually, desperately, pray for my son to be healed from his chronic illness, and sometimes for healing from mine, too.

This brings us to Zechariah's prayer. Zechariah's priestly division, Abijah, would only serve in the temple twice a year, and there were approximately 750 other priests within his division to choose from each time. With those statistics, making the incense offering was a once-in-a-lifetime honour. God worked through a lottery to engineer the temple encounter.

When the angel appears, he says to Zechariah, 'Your prayer has been heard' (v. 13). But which prayer? It is highly unlikely that Zechariah was still praying for a child; after all, they were both old and that opportunity had passed. The aorist tense in Greek suggests this is not an ongoing prayer but a one-off prayer, perhaps when Zechariah prostrated himself on the altar that day. This is the peak of his calling, and from the temple this righteous man would be praying for the redemption of Israel. He likely prayed for the world, not himself.

The way God answered that prayer, therefore, was beautiful. For years, Zechariah had prayed for a child, but for centuries, the people of God pleaded for Israel's redemption. Finally, the time was now: God would indeed redeem Israel and prepare the people for the Lord's coming (v. 17). But God answered the general prayer by also honouring Zechariah's personal desire. Through John, God would bring rejoicing generally to the 'many', and 'joy and delight' to Zechariah specifically (v. 14).

This is not a guarantee that if we pray for world peace God will grant all our wishes as a reward. Prayer is more complicated than a formula. Rather, this passage speaks of the character of God, who loves the world in general and loves you specifically. God is not indifferent to our loss or shame, and longs to give us delight and joy. This is the God we worship.

## Reflect

- In your prayer life, what is the balance between global concerns and your personal ones?
- What difference does it make to know that God hears all prayers and longs to bring joy?
- How does Zechariah's story encourage you to keep praying when God is silent?

## Pray

*O God who hears our half-uttered longings,*
*we bring you today the big and the small,*
*the general and the personal,*
*world peace and candied fruit,*
*knowing you love to bring your people joy.*
*Amen.*

# 7 December

## Zechariah loses his voice

**Zechariah asked the angel, 'How can I be sure of this? I am an old man and my wife is well on in years.'**

**The angel said to him, 'I am Gabriel. I stand in the presence of God, and I have been sent to speak to you and to tell you this good news. And now you will be silent and not able to speak until the day this happens, because you did not believe my words, which will come true at their appointed time.'**

**Meanwhile, the people were waiting for Zechariah and wondering why he stayed so long in the temple. When he came out, he could not speak to them. They realised he had seen a vision in the temple, for he kept making signs to them but remained unable to speak.**

LUKE 1:18–22

There are three things you should know about Dave: first, he loves his job teaching the Hebrew Bible in a seminary in the US; second, he loves coaching soccer and basketball teams, and third, he is an extrovert with a powerful, loud voice.[8] This is why, when he damaged his vocal cords and lost his voice for several months, Dave found it one of the worst experiences of his life.

Not only did it affect his work and hobbies, but it also changed how he interacted with people. Losing your voice can force an extrovert into behaving like a shy introvert, and people start responding to you accordingly, which in turn shapes your own identity. It is an extraordinarily humbling thing.

Zechariah's punishment for not believing an angel was to 'not be able to speak' until the day Gabriel's words came true (v. 20). The word describing his mutism is *kōphos*, which can mean mute, deaf, or both. Given that Luke 1:62 mentions others making signs to Zechariah, not just him signing to them (v. 22), the third option is most likely.

Although God's people across the ages have believed that disability is punishment for sin, the instances of God using illness or disability as discipline are rare, usually time-limited, and the people receiving it know very clearly which specific sin occasioned it. Two such examples are Miriam's temporary skin disease (Numbers 12) and Jeroboam's momentarily shrivelled hand (1 Kings 13). Jesus consistently contradicted the assumption that disability was caused by sin or a punishment from God (e.g. John 9:1–3; Luke 13:1–3). If you are disabled, as I am, please be reassured that unless you also have a message from the angel Gabriel himself saying otherwise, it is not punishment from God.

On one level, Zechariah's treatment seems unfair. Zechariah's question clearly echoes Abram's, who was also old and childless: 'How can I know...?' (Genesis 15:8). Abram received reassurance from the Lord, not rebuke. Sometimes I muse that Gabriel was just having a particularly long, bad day. Gabriel's threefold statement, 'I am Gabriel', 'I stand in the presence of God', and 'I have been sent [from God]' positively drips with exasperation at being disrespected (v. 19).

Gabriel's issues aside, it is perhaps precisely because of Abram's earlier doubt that Zechariah has less excuse for doubt now. How could Zechariah believe in a miraculous pregnancy after years of infertility? Because God had done it before: for Abraham and Sarah (Genesis 21:1–5); for Rebekah (Genesis 25:21); Rachel (Genesis 30:22–23); Samson's mother (Judges 13); and for Hannah (1 Samuel 1). Whenever we are tempted to doubt that God can ever bring miracles in our own lives, it's good to remember that the Lord has plenty of experience in that field already.

There is no question that nine months of silence was difficult for Zechariah, as it was for Dave. And yet, I also see the wry, loving grace of God in it: Zechariah's request for a guarantee was answered. During those long months, as he watched his wife's belly burgeon, his continued mutism was a reassurance that God would indeed give him a son for the redemption of Israel. His 'punishment' was also a gift. He lost his voice, but he gained a sign.

While Zechariah's situation was unique, God's unchanging, loving grace is a universal comfort. I give thanks for the possibility of divine miracles that defy our expectations, and I lean on God's ongoing grace towards wavering doubters.

## Reflect and pray

- First, bring to mind all the important issues dear to your heart that you wish God could solve. To express any doubt, you could use Zechariah's experience to mirror your own feelings.

  *Lord, I am gripped with fear* (Luke 1:12).
  *Lord, I want to be sure* (Luke 1:18).

- Second, reflect on similar situations within the Bible.

  *Lord, you healed the sick; provided for the needy; rescued the vulnerable; saved the oppressed; mended broken relationships; made miracles happen. Please do this for me.*

- Third, pray about each of your seemingly impossible situations. You can use this phrase to express your commitment to trusting God.

  *Lord, while life is uncertain, I choose to trust in your loving grace.*

# 8 December

## Elizabeth loses her disgrace

**When his time of service was completed, he returned home. After this his wife Elizabeth became pregnant and for five months remained in seclusion. 'The Lord has done this for me,' she said. 'In these days he has shown his favour and taken away my disgrace among the people.'**

LUKE 1:23–25

How does our society view older women? To find out, Sue Westwood, a researcher at the University of York, asked 158 women over the age of 50.[9]

'Frankly,' one 71-year-old woman responded, 'it's the not being seen that is most tiresome.'

What Westwood discovered was that older women are typically not 'seen', not served in shop queues, not called upon in public meetings, and talked over by younger people. When older women *are* seen, they are only valued for their former procreation and therefore labelled as 'grandmother' (even when they're not a grandmother), whereas older men tend to be labelled by their former work titles.

So perhaps our culture is not quite so different from Elizabeth's day than we might expect.

Today's passage is short, but it packs a punch. The first part of Elizabeth's pregnancy is characterised by silence. When Zechariah returned from his service in Jerusalem, he was mute and possibly deaf. We are also told that Elizabeth spends the first five months of her pregnancy in seclusion – perhaps because she wanted to be cautious about spreading the good news too early, or to protect the baby, or because she had pregnancy sickness. Whatever the reason, it may well have been a secret between her, Zechariah, and God.

Elizabeth's immediate reaction, unlike Zechariah's, was thankfulness to God. But it's her language that's surprising; rather than thanking God straightforwardly for a son, she thanks God for showing 'favour' and erasing her 'disgrace among the people' (Luke 1:25).

The more I think about that word, 'disgrace', the sadder I feel for Elizabeth, who bore for years that yearning to be accepted like a dagger in her soul. In the Jewish honour–shame culture, honour had different nuances, according to gender. Though there were exceptions, generally a man was recognised as honourable through courage, leadership, social status, and wisdom, whereas honour for a woman was often solely awarded for modesty, motherhood, and purity.[10]

God saw and celebrated Elizabeth and Zechariah as righteous and obedient people, yet the crowd disrespected Elizabeth for being childless. It's such a natural desire to be seen by others and honoured for who we are that even when we know God loves us, we still yearn for acceptance from others.

There are so many Elizabeths today who similarly feel that they have spent their whole life on the edge of society, being rejected for something over which they have no control. Maybe you've also known that pain of inexplicable rejection and it tugs at your heart today.

Elizabeth rejoiced because God had given her a way of being accepted according to the standards of her society: bearing a child. Yet, if we dig deeper, we can see God's bigger, better vision for women as the early church develops. Prior to Jesus' coming, with notable exceptions, such as Miriam, Deborah, and Jael, the women of the Bible were mentioned for their role as mothers or wives. But in the early church, women are given a wider variety of labels: Junia, the apostle; Lydia, the businesswoman; Priscilla, the teacher of apostles; Dorcas, the charity worker; Phoebe, the deacon. Even Lois and Eunice, Timothy's grandmother and mother, are given special mention by Paul for their faith, and they are honoured for their impressive child-rearing, not simply their child-bearing.

In fact, when we next see Elizabeth, she will be prophesying. Elizabeth's longing, like many of ours, was to be accepted by her society, yet God, with an abundance of love, had even greater honour in store for her. If today, you are feeling disrespected by society or feel like you don't belong, remember that God's honour system is greater and fairer than anything this world has to offer.

## Reflect

- In what ways do you yearn to be honoured – or seen differently – by family and friends?
- In what ways do you feel 'unseen' by society?

## Pray

*Dear Lord,*
*You are the God who sees.*
*Thank you for seeing me, while others ignore.*
*Thank you for honouring me, while others deplore.*
*Lift my eyes to you, I pray.*
*Amen.*

# 9 December

## Mary finds favour

**In the sixth month of Elizabeth's pregnancy, God sent the angel Gabriel to Nazareth, a town in Galilee, to a virgin pledged to be married to a man named Joseph, a descendant of David. The virgin's name was Mary. The angel went to her and said, 'Greetings, you who are highly favoured! The Lord is with you.'**

**Mary was greatly troubled at his words and wondered what kind of greeting this might be. But the angel said to her, 'Do not be afraid, Mary, you have found favour with God.'**

LUKE 1:26–30

I wonder how God the Father, Son, and Holy Spirit decided on who should be entrusted with parenting Jesus. If I were an angel advising them, I would suggest the Messiah be born into an impressive family, perhaps of King David's lineage or priestly heritage, so he would be taken seriously. The parents should be married, respected in the community, perhaps leaders themselves, so Jesus would automatically be well thought-of when he began his ministry. And – perhaps most importantly – God-as-baby must be protected at all costs, educated with every advantage, well-fed, and safe from all danger. The stakes are surely too high for anything else.

This raises the question: why did God the Trinity choose Mary as Jesus' mother? John the Baptist's father, Zechariah, had some honour and status as a priest, a respected family line, and an impeccable public record of righteousness. His call came in Israel's capital, in the holy place, at a moment of spiritual importance for the people of God.

It makes sense to choose Zechariah to be a parent of such an important prophet.

Yet as Luke continues the story, we travel northwards from the great Jerusalem metropolis towards a more remote, rural, and obscure region, Galilee, and the small town of Nazareth, commonly derided as a backwater hole where losers live (John 1:46). There, we zoom in on a probably teenage girl, with no special family or pedigree, who is engaged but not yet married. The betrothal was a serious agreement, with a dowry given in return for the guarantee of marriage. After about a year, the groom would take his bride home, where they would consummate the marriage. This is all we know about her.

Surely there could not be a more unlikely choice for Gabriel's visitation. Angelic visits to women were extremely rare, and God announced miracle babies to both Abram and Zechariah rather than their wives. As far as societal status went, Mary was low on the list: young, female, and poor, her family unworthy of mention.

In a world where honour and reputation are everything, Jesus chooses Mary and gives up the opportunity to be born into privilege. Jesus chooses Mary, along with risk, poverty, and obscurity. Mary is given favour; Jesus loses prestige.

Whatever metrics we have for measuring human worth, God takes delight in utterly defying them. Before God, Mary is one who is 'highly favoured' (v. 28). That is her descriptor, her characterising feature. In fact, Gabriel repeats it, for emphasis and reassurance: 'You have found favour with God' (v. 30).

God offers no justification or explanation for Mary's call, no spiritually impressive CV of prophecy, miracles, or good deeds is presented. We only know this: while most of us run around chasing respect, power, riches, or meaning, God quietly honours ordinary people unnoticed by others. When the world ignores you, remember that you are God's favourite.

## Reflect

- What makes you tempted to feel ordinary or insignificant?
- 1 Peter 5:5 says that God 'shows favour to the humble'. How do you react to this?

## Pray

*Lord Jesus,*
*Thank you that you do not play the world's games*
*or measure with the world's yard sticks.*
*Thank you for showing me favour.*
*Please help me notice the beauty of ordinary people*
*and show honour to all.*
*Amen.*

# 10 December

## Mary risks her reputation

**'You will conceive and give birth to a son, and you are to call him Jesus. He will be great and will be called the Son of the Most High. The Lord God will give him the throne of his father David, and he will reign over Jacob's descendants forever; his kingdom will never end.'**

**'How will this be,' Mary asked the angel, 'since I am a virgin?'**

**The angel answered, 'The Holy Spirit will come on you, and the power of the Most High will overshadow you. So the holy one to be born will be called the Son of God...'**

**'I am the Lord's servant,' Mary answered. 'May your word to me be fulfilled.' Then the angel left her.**

LUKE 1:31–35, 38

A month before D-Day, the Allied forces were desperate for intelligence on Nazi plans. Several male spies had just been caught and killed, so Britain tried something different. They sent in a young woman.

Phyllis Latour posed as a teenage girl, cycling around and selling soap to German soldiers, chatting with them and casually asking where their units were based. She sent daily reports via wireless. The codes she needed were all on pieces of silk. One time, a code was hidden in a flat shoelace tying up her hair. There was a tense moment when a female soldier ordered she be strip-searched, then looked closely at her hair. Concealing her nerves, Phyllis breezily grabbed the lace herself, undid the knot and shook out her hair. The soldier waved her through.

Because of her youth and femininity, Phyllis was overlooked – and underestimated. As a result, she was successful where others had failed.[11]

Phyllis shares some similarities with Mary. As we reflect on the miracle of Mary's pregnancy, we often miss the fact that she was hand-picked for a life-threatening mission.

If only Gabriel had come a few months later, it would have been simple. She would be married to Joseph, David's descendant, having slept with him, and they would together be given a child who was clearly the long-awaited Messiah. 'Son of God' (Luke 1:35) was a common honorific title for kings of Israel, especially David and Solomon, and the prophets had foretold of a great king who would sit on David's throne forever.

There is, however, a sting in the tail. As Gabriel talks, Mary begins to twig that the 'conception' will not be after her marriage to Joseph, but immediately, while she is still a virgin. Her question, 'How will this be…?' (v. 34) is not an expression of doubt, as Zechariah's question was, but trying to clarify Gabriel's meaning. With all God's miracles in Israel's past, this one was unprecedented.

What would this mean for her? While modern day retellings emphasise her vulnerability as a teenager, perhaps 15, giving birth at an earlier age was not abnormal in her day. The problem was getting pregnant before her betrothal was consummated in marriage.

Who would believe that this was a miracle rather than garden-variety infidelity? Mary, venerated for centuries afterwards as an icon of virginity, in her own day risked being despised for promiscuity.

This would not just affect her but would rain disgrace upon her entire family. In an honour–shame culture, that is everything. Her father would be publicly ridiculed or shunned and the extended family would also be tainted. This event would also be seen as a challenge to Joseph's honour, challenging his masculinity. One way for Joseph or her father to recover their honour would be to order Mary's death by stoning. We know that punishment was still practised in Jesus' day (John 8:1–8), just as so-called 'honour-killings' still happen in our world today.

Sometimes our callings are pure joy and delight, making our soul come alive. Other times, God calls believers to missions that risk ridicule, hatred or – in desperate times – even our own life. When hatred is the political currency, even the call to love everyone with justice for all can be interpreted as sedition.

How much of all that entered Mary's mind as Gabriel explained the deal to her is something we cannot know. Yet surely Mary's declaration, 'May your word to me be fulfilled' (v. 38) is not a naive, submissive nod but a courageous acceptance to a terrifying commission. It is not her meekness but her boldness that challenges me.

## Reflect

- Have you ever been given a task that felt overwhelming?
- How does Mary's courage inspire you?

## Pray

*O Lord,*
*when I fear the cost of doing the right thing,*
*give me the boldness of Mary,*
*the seal of your favour,*
*and the power of your Spirit.*
*Amen.*

# 11 December

## Mary is given support

**'Even Elizabeth your relative is going to have a child in her old age, and she who was said to be unable to conceive is in her sixth month. For no word from God will ever fail.'**

**'I am the Lord's servant,' Mary answered. 'May your word to me be fulfilled.' Then the angel left her.**

**At that time Mary got ready and hurried to a town in the hill country of Judea, where she entered Zechariah's home and greeted Elizabeth.**

LUKE 1:36–40

God first awarded Mary favour, then handed her the task of raising a child without a human father. This was surely a bittersweet call, and a lonely one, as Joseph's rejection of her was a reasonable assumption. But then God gave her Elizabeth.

We assume that Mary was living in her father's house, and as we have seen, that may have been dangerous for her. But if anyone were to believe that God could create a virginal conception, it was someone who knew their own pregnancy was a miracle. This is perhaps why Mary left immediately – 'at that time' – and 'hurried' to Judea (Luke 1:39). If Mary was beginning to fear for her safety, God provided her with a sanctuary.

If Mary were tempted to doubt her own pregnancy in those early days, through Elizabeth she would daily know the physicality of the miraculous, the ethereal made fleshy, the supernatural made natural.

When Elizabeth came to give birth, with all the fear and danger that entailed, Mary would be with her, a visual reminder that God can do the impossible. When either of them saw one another, they would remember, 'For no word from God will ever fail' (v. 37).

At the age of 23, my friend Elizabeth moved into a Bristol suburb for her work, where she attended a small church. Without many people her age, she struck up a friendship with Margaret, who was 80 and recently widowed. Together, they went out in the evenings to the cinema or theatre, chatting away at the end of the night.

Margaret was delighted: she felt frustrated with friends her own age who went to bed early (and judged her for lying in till noon). After moving around a lot, Elizabeth appreciated Margaret's solidity and stability, the particular wisdom that comes from living a long time in one place. Most of all, Elizabeth was inspired by Margaret's rebellious spirit and the idea of doing older age in an unconventional way.

They may have seemed like an unusual pairing, but God brought them both together. Their intergenerational friendship enriched them both. Margaret was provided with much-needed distraction after her husband died, and Elizabeth went on to be a clinical psychologist who specialises in supporting older people's mental health.

There have been times in my life that have felt almost impossible but for the love of family and friends. When we are tempted to wobble in our faith or resolve, we need others who can support us, understand us, and point us to God. Friends are God's gift to us for sanctuary, sanity, and resilience.

## Reflect

- Intergenerational friendships are rare, but more likely to find in the context of church. What positive intergenerational friendships have you encountered?
- Who are your 'soul friends'?
- Whom might God be asking you to support?

## Review

- Having seen how honour and shame affected Jesus' society, how does that compare with our society today?
- Zechariah, Elizabeth, and Mary all faced some degree of social shame but divine honour. How does this change how you see yourself or others?

## Pray

*Lord Jesus,*
*friend of sinners and disciples and us,*
*in your goodness, bless us with friendships,*
*for rainy days and parking fines,*
*for exam results and exciting news,*
*for turning mountains back into molehills,*
*for walking with us when the path is unclear.*
*Give me kindred spirits filled with your Holy Spirit;*
*place your wisdom into the mouths of my companions,*
*show me your love made tangible in a hug.*
*Give me friends, I pray.*
*Amen.*

# 3

# Songs after silence

# Introduction

## Three Christmases

### Christmas one

On Christmas Day 2022, Bekah had a smile on her face as her family celebrated together, but her stomach carried a rock of dread and a whirlpool of sadness. Her beloved husband, Steve, had just been told that there were no more treatment options for his cancer. Steve had reacted with his characteristic relentless optimism, but Bekah realised this meant it was most likely months, not years, that Steve had remaining. Not wanting to burst Steve's bubble or spoil Christmas for their grown-up kids, she said nothing to the family. She held that secret in self-imposed silence, all the while thinking during each present-unwrapping and cracker-pulling, 'This could be our last Christmas together.'

### Christmas two

In April 2023, Steve was officially told he likely had five months left to live, and with dark humour, they marked the date of his death as 17 September. But by the time that date came, Steve was feeling remarkably well, and they realised they'd have another Christmas together, after all. In that case, Bekah decided, they were going to go all out and make this the best Christmas possible.

With their blended family of grown-up children, some of whom also had partners, they usually couldn't get everyone together, but that year, all the children were under the same roof, and they welcomed a new grandchild, too. They held a big party for all their friends and saw extended family. There were unexpected blessings too: they were given tickets for a 'proper big fat Christmas service' put on by the Salvation Army in the Royal Albert Hall, and tickets to Jools Holland's *Annual Hootenanny*, and each week in December they went to a beautiful, musical carol service that inspired them to rejoice in Christ's coming. The touchstones of family tradition were repeated, with each of them making gingerbread men and decorating them together, with much laughter.

## Christmas three

On 16 September 2024, Steve succumbed to his cancer, almost exactly a year after he 'should' have died. Someone had told Bekah that she would never enjoy Christmas again now she was a widow, but Bekah determined that Christmas would still be joyful, despite the pain of missing Steve. Though the first Christmas without Steve was hard, and the whole family felt the loss, they still made gingerbread men together, laughed, and celebrated Jesus' birth.

# Silences

In this life, there are different types of silences, and most of them are bad. Silences can be individual or communal; some people-groups, countries or communities are routinely ignored while others are given a megaphone. There are dark silences, when we live in fear but cannot speak; jittery silences, when we fear that someone will guess our secret; panicked silences, when we cannot speak because we know we won't be believed; white silences, when we just don't have the words; watery silences of private loss and tears shed alone; forced silences, when we have spoken then been punished, ridiculed, or shunned. There are silences of unbearable limbo and silences of deep grief. The release and relief of having a safe place to speak honestly after those silences cannot be understated.

In the nativity story, we see the painful long silence of infertility, Mary's panicked silence when she runs to Elizabeth, Zechariah's temporary silence as he waited to see if he could trust God's word, and the silence of God for almost 400 years after the last minor prophet had predicted that the Messiah would come.

There are also good silences: when we are moved to awe by nature or art; the comforting silence of being with someone who understands; the silence of prayer as God fills the space with love; the hush of a theatre before the curtain goes up and the seconds of silent appreciation from the audience just before they thunder in applause; and Mary, pondering all those amazing promises.

Whatever silences – or silencing – we have experienced, it is good to know that God doesn't leave us there. After silence, there is always a song.

## Songs

I asked Bekah what song, if any, she felt God had given her to sing.

'After the silence of my fear,' she said slowly, 'we had that unexpected, wonderful "bonus" year together, with a joyful Christmas. That time for me was a time of singing and being so grateful to God. Even when Steve died, that song continued, despite the sadness. In the time of silence and the three years of Steve's illness, God had time to work on me and in me, so that by the end of it, I missed Steve more than I can say, but I'm insanely grateful for having him as long as I did.

'My first marriage was awful, so I've always had a real appreciation of the good. I'm not a saint, but I've never been cross at God for Steve's death, because I was given a great love, and so many others don't have that. I was silent for a long time as I held a lot inside, but what I've been left with is a song – a song of gratitude.'

Whatever you are holding today, remember that God's goodness ultimately wins. After the silence, there is always a song, even if you don't yet know what it will be. Some songs are of praise, gratitude, joy, and wonder. Others are lament, plea, or prophetic protest, and these are important too. As you read this section, consider the silences you hold within you and the songs God has given you to sing.

# 12 December

## Elizabeth is given a song of wonder

**When Elizabeth heard Mary's greeting, the baby leaped in her womb, and Elizabeth was filled with the Holy Spirit. In a loud voice she exclaimed: 'Blessed are you among women, and blessed is the child you will bear! But why am I so favoured, that the mother of my Lord should come to me? As soon as the sound of your greeting reached my ears, the baby in my womb leaped for joy. Blessed is she who has believed that the Lord would fulfil his promises to her!'...**

**Mary stayed with Elizabeth for about three months and then returned home.**

LUKE 1:41–45, 56

If I were to ask a roomful of church ministers who was the first person to recognise Jesus as the Messiah (God's chosen king), what would their answer be? My bet would be Peter, because of his reply to Jesus' question, 'Who do you say I am?' (e.g. Luke 9:20).

But Peter wasn't the first: it was Elizabeth.[12]

Elizabeth is criminally overlooked and under-celebrated as far as saints go. She and her son are the first people in the gospels to be 'filled with the Holy Spirit' (v. 41) and hers is the first human voice to prophesy about Jesus. When she sees Mary, she is given sudden, supernatural insight – not only is Mary barely pregnant, but her baby is 'my Lord', which can mean my God, master, or king. As the Messiah would turn out to be not only God's chosen king but God in essence, this title was remarkably prescient. Elizabeth declares God's blessing on Mary and God's blessing on Jesus, still in the womb (v. 42). We should pause here: Elizabeth blessed Jesus, the source of all blessing – it is mind-blowing.

Elizabeth is not only a prophet but also a first-rate cheerleader. In my previous book, *Those Who Wait* (Malcolm Down Publishing, 2017), I imagined Mary's journey to Elizabeth, full of fear about how she would tell of her pregnancy and whether she would be believed. Elizabeth's greeting means that before Mary has even uttered a word, she knows that she will not have to explain, let alone justify, her pregnancy.

A pettier person, realising that Mary was pregnant with a miracle baby, might have been annoyed that Mary was stealing her thunder, just when Elizabeth was shaping up to be Sarah 2.0. Elizabeth, though, is humble – 'Why am I so favoured…?' (v. 43) – and just bursts with delight and blessing for Mary. She has herself been blessed, and she rushes to bless others. There's no hesitation, no shadow of suspicion, judgement, or envy, just gushing, loud, prophetic encouragement.

Meanwhile, the relationship of the two miracle mothers is paralleled by the children in their wombs. John the Baptist, still embryonic, leaps for joy as Jesus, merely a few cells dividing at this stage, enters the room. Elizabeth recognises this as a prophetic movement reacting to the Messiah's arrival. Elizabeth is Mary's cheerleader, John the Baptist will be Jesus' forerunner, and what a gift they both were to the holy family.

The impact on Mary is significant, as we see in the next verses. Encouraging words and prophetic insight are so powerful that they can often carry us through hard times. Mary stayed for three months of reassurance, until Elizabeth's baby was born safely and Mary's own pregnancy was showing.

Elizabeth's role of cheerleader was a gift to Mary, but it was also God's gift to Elizabeth. Even in the reading of it we sense Elizabeth's overwhelming joy. Whenever we are like Elizabeth, recognising the presence of Jesus in other people and celebrating it, we are not only giving something precious, but receiving it ourselves. To be an encourager is not only to give a gift but to get one.

## Reflect

- Consider: in whom do you delight simply for the person they are?
- Which people inspire you because of God's work in and through them? How might you encourage them today?
- What is your 'song of wonder' for today?

## Pray

Pray today for those who might need some encouragement and affirmation.

*Dear Lord God,*
*like Elizabeth,*
*may I be filled with your Spirit*
*and spur others on;*
*like John the Baptist,*
*may I always leap for joy*
*at the prospect of your arrival.*
*Amen.*

## Sing

A challenge: this week, try to find time every day to sing. The physiological benefits of singing are well-established, and this can help calm our nervous systems as December gets more frantic. God has designed our bodies for song, and singing praise also ministers to our soul.

Today's suggestion: 'What child is this?' (W. Chatterton Dix, 1837–98), to the tune of 'Greensleeves'.

# 13 December

## Mary is given a song of joy

**And Mary said:**
**'My soul glorifies the Lord**
**and my spirit rejoices in God my Saviour,**
**for he has been mindful**
**of the humble state of his servant.**
**From now on all generations will call me blessed,**
**for the Mighty One has done great things for me –**
**holy is his name.'**
LUKE 1:46–49

After Elizabeth honoured her, Mary could have been smug about her own importance. Yet Mary doesn't even thank Elizabeth for the compliment but takes that honour and bounces it straight back up to God. When it says, 'My soul glorifies the Lord', the verb is literally to make bigger: the Greek word contains 'mega'. She is utterly sincere in her gratitude.

Mary thanks God for two things – noticing her 'humble state' and then doing 'great things' for her (Luke 1:48–49). When people talk about being blessed by God on social media today, often they mean they have been granted riches, success, or fame. This is not the blessing for which Mary is grateful. She is poor and will remain so. She is young, as yet unmarried, and for all she knows, she may still be in danger.

It's almost as though Elizabeth's prophetic exclamation has taken away the veil so she can glimpse the heavenly reality and see the world through God's eyes. She is filled with joy, and the object of her joy is ‘God my Saviour’, ‘the Lord’, ‘the Mighty One’ – over and over, she names him and thanks him.

Sheila Akomiah-Conteh has a song like Mary’s. Born in Ghana, seeing herself as very ordinary, she never imagined that God would call her to be a highly respected research fellow in theology for the University of Aberdeen and a leader in the largest church of her denomination. She can relate to Mary’s joy.

‘For me, as an African Christian,’ she explained, ‘this passage shows that God is no respecter of either wealth or non-wealth but a respecter of people, whoever they are.’ As God blessed Mary in her ‘humble state’, so today God is quietly blessing faithful believers whom society overlooks.

‘A lot of Africans resonate with the inclusion that the gospel invites and exemplifies – especially inclusion for those the world would consider poor or lowly,’ Sheila explained. ‘God can bring people from the margins to be the superstars.’[13]

In the rest of her song, Mary will praise God for what this means for everyone else, but first she stops to thank God for her own blessing. She gets to be a part of God’s plan. God has noticed her in particular, as well as hearing the cries of the world in general.

We can hold this together: the personal with the universal. We can rejoice in general for God’s love for the world. Yet God also blesses individuals, notices those who think they are too lowly to really matter, and makes those on the margins superstars in God’s kingdom. I can both thank God for saving the world and thank God for loving me. The Lord has done great things for me: holy is his name.

## Reflect and pray

As you consider all that Jesus has done for us in general and you personally, try praying Mary's prayer as your own, meditating on each phrase.

*My soul glorifies –*
*magnifies, increases*
*the Lord –*

*and my spirit rejoices*
*in God my Saviour –*

*all generations will call me blessed –*

*because*
*the Mighty One*

*has done great things for me.*

*Holy is his name.*

*Holy is your name, O Lord.*
*You have done great things for me.*
*You make my soul rejoice.*

Alternatively, use Psalm 13, a song of lament, as your prayer.

## Sing

'Joy to the world' (Isaac Watts, 1674–1748, music 'Antioch' by Lowell Mason, 1792–1872).

# 14 December

## The hungry are given good things

**'His mercy extends to those who fear him,**
**from generation to generation.**
**He has performed mighty deeds with his arm;**
**he has scattered those who are proud in their inmost thoughts.**
**He has brought down rulers from their thrones**
**but has lifted up the humble.**
**He has filled the hungry with good things**
**but has sent the rich away empty.'**

LUKE 1:50–53

If Elizabeth is overlooked as a prophet, then surely Mary is even more. Most portraits of Mary paint her in pastel colours, passive and serene, but there is one artist who truly captures her prophetic side. Ben Wildflower made a black and white woodcut print of Mary as a defiant revolutionary, fist raised in the air and boot-clad feet trampling a skull and a snake (representing death and evil). The words around her read, 'Cast down the mighty', 'Send the rich away', 'Fill the hungry', and 'Lift the lowly'. When Christians complained about the politicisation of Mary in his piece, Ben had to point out that these were words from the Bible.

Mary's song declares what Jesus will do. It is no less than a complete overthrow of society: the proud are scattered, but the poor are brought near; the rich are left empty, but the hungry are filled; the rulers are humbled, and the humble are lifted. Although in one sense the Bible is beyond politics, God is always deeply concerned with social justice in the here and now, not just future spiritual rewards. God does take sides and, throughout the Bible, shows favour to the poor and oppressed.

One phrase I have always stumbled over is, 'He has filled the hungry with good things' (v. 53). As a young child, I saw images of starving Ethiopian children in the early 1980s, which prompted the much-critiqued pop song questioning whether they knew it was Christmastime. Was this promise to the hungry only for Jesus' second coming?

Sheila Akomiah-Conteh, a Ghanaian theologian living in Scotland, helped me understand how the passage is usually interpreted in African theology (noting that not everyone in the continent of Africa is poor, and some are very rich indeed).

'The "good things" are more spiritual than physical,' she said. Her father lives in a village where everyone has very little, but everyone shares their crops, goes to church, and praises God together, and generally they are joyful.

'If you give them more, they're happy to receive, but they have the joy of the Lord,' she explained. 'It's enough. You can be hungry and praise God. You can be filled spiritually.'

Manny Mvula, a Zambian Christian conservationist who grew up in a rural African village, sees the west as so obsessed with wealth that we lose out on greater blessings. He said emphatically that poorer Africans aren't sitting passively waiting for Jesus to return or for the west to rescue them; rather, they are seeing God's provision daily. He smiled at me knowingly: 'The promise of the Bible is that the poor will come first. We know [from experience] that God is faithful and wants to adorn us with blessings.' Mary's prophecy is for today.

Alfred Sebahene, a Tanzanian public theologian, acknowledged that African suffering and issues of corruption are a real concern. However, most African communities reflect biblical values to mitigate this.

'African community speaks of "we" and not "I". This king is not the individual king. This is *our* king,' Alfred said. 'If I am well, that means my community is well. If one is suffering, we say we must do something together.'

What this means in practice is sacrificial sharing so that all may thrive. Everyone in the village knows which families have enjoyed a good harvest that year, and the hungry will go there. Yet this is not seen as handouts but mutual gift-giving. Everyone brings something whenever they visit, according to what you have – perhaps a single mango or some bananas – and you also go home with a gift.

'This doesn't always mean that where you're taking the maize they are hungry – and you may return with a basket of their own maize!' Alfred explained. In a gift-giving culture that rejoices in God, there are always material and spiritual gifts flowing in abundance.[14]

This is why the word of God needs to be interpreted by the global people of God, past and present. Jesus came to fill the hungry with good things. Yet Christ's blessings are often mediated through Christ's body, the church. Jesus still calls us all to feed the hungry, lift the lowly and give to the poor. We need to do globally what these African villages do locally: share sacrificially so that all may thrive.

Nevertheless, Mary's song offers us a deeper message. Spiritual riches, not material goods, are what mark us out as blessed.

## Reflect

- How does the witness of these African theologians encourage or challenge you?
- What might God be calling you to give or receive?
- What 'song of social justice' has God given you to sing?

## Pray

*Dear Lord, please fill the hungry with good things, and may I be a part of that.*

## Sing

'O holy night' (lyrics Placide Cappeau, 1808–77; English translation John Sullivan Dwight, 1813–93; music Adolphe Adam, 1803–56).

# 15 December

## Zechariah is given a tongue of praise

**When it was time for Elizabeth to have her baby, she gave birth to a son. Her neighbours and relatives heard that the Lord had shown her great mercy, and they shared her joy.**

**On the eighth day they came to circumcise the child, and they were going to name him after his father Zechariah, but his mother spoke up and said, 'No! He is to be called John.'**

**They said to her, 'There is no one among your relatives who has that name.'**

**Then they made signs to his father, to find out what he would like to name the child. He asked for a writing tablet, and to everyone's astonishment he wrote, 'His name is John.' Immediately his mouth was opened and his tongue set free, and he began to speak, praising God. All the neighbours were filled with awe, and throughout the hill country of Judea people were talking about all these things. Everyone who heard this wondered about it, asking, 'What then is this child going to be?' For the Lord's hand was with him.**

**His father Zechariah was filled with the Holy Spirit and prophesied.**

LUKE 1:57–67

While we may remember that Zechariah temporarily lost his voice after he doubted Gabriel, we may have forgotten when he was supposed to get his voice back. Gabriel had promised, 'Your wife Elizabeth will bear you a son, *and* you are to call him John' (Luke 1:13, italics added), and then he explained that Zechariah would not speak 'until the day this happens' (Luke 1:20).

I don't know about you, but if I were Zechariah, I would expect to get my voice back on the day I became a father. The baby was born, the prophecy fulfilled. But that didn't happen. He was still mute, with no certainty about ever speaking again.

To be a faithful Jew, you must circumcise all sons on the eighth day. Although Jews in Zechariah's day named children at birth, Elizabeth and Zechariah chose to wait until circumcision to name their son, meaning all the neighbours were in attendance.

I love Luke's feminist humour in highlighting that Elizabeth already knew her baby's God-appointed name. It was, however, the right of the father to name a child. The detail of Zechariah asking for a tablet, likely a piece of wood covered in wax, hints at how Zechariah would have communicated without speech over the previous nine months.

It was only at the point that Zechariah declared, 'His name is John' (v. 64), fulfilling the final detail of Gabriel's prophecy, that God restored Zechariah's voice. Two responses are worth noting: Zechariah's and the neighbours'. We had last seen Zechariah with cynicism and doubt, even when faced with an angel of God, but now he spills over with praise. During those nine months of silence, God had apparently been at work, and now Zechariah was transformed.

In addition to praising God, he prophesied. This is a reminder that God delights in giving us second chances. Though Zechariah previously doubted, whereas Mary believed, both were later filled with the Spirit and became prophets. If we fear that we have failed God in the past, God is there, bringing transformation, forgiveness – and grace upon grace. God gives doubters a chance (and second chances) to become ministers.

Even God's delay, which must have caused Zechariah considerable anxiety, had a purpose. The neighbours witnessed Zechariah's miraculous healing and were in awe of God. The public nature of the miracle added credibility to the private promise that John would be significant in God's kingdom. John may well have needed that reassurance for his future ministry.

I have been through long periods where not my tongue but my soul felt silenced, and God felt absent. I don't always understand God's timing or purpose in this. Yet I also know something of the subtle transformation that occurs in these times, and I am grateful for it. Today, if you struggle with doubt, remember Zechariah's transformation.

## Reflect

- Have you ever been grateful in retrospect for a delay in your plans?
- Where does your soul feel silenced right now? Where are you finding joy?
- What song of transformation, second chances, or grace to doubters has God given you to sing?

## Pray

*Lord, bear with us doubters and have mercy on all who have lost the sense of your presence. Transform us, fill us with your Spirit, and give us a joyful song, we pray. Amen.*

## Sing

'O, for a thousand tongues to sing' (Charles Wesley, 1707–88, music 'Azmon', Carl Gläser, arranged by Lowell Mason, 1792–1872).

## 16 December

# We are given salvation and forgiveness

**'Praise be to the Lord, the God of Israel,**
**because he has come to his people and redeemed them.**
**He has raised up a horn of salvation for us**
**in the house of his servant David**
**(as he said through his holy prophets of long ago),**
**salvation from our enemies**
**and from the hand of all who hate us –**
**to show mercy to our ancestors**
**and to remember his holy covenant,**
**the oath he swore to our father Abraham:**
**to rescue us from the hand of our enemies,**
**and to enable us to serve him without fear**
**in holiness and righteousness before him all our days.**

**And you, my child, will be called a prophet of the Most High;**
**for you will go on before the Lord to prepare the way for him,**
**to give his people the knowledge of salvation**
**through the forgiveness of their sins.**

LUKE 1:68–77

Zechariah breaks nine months of silence by blessing God for breaking centuries of silence. There had been no major prophecy (after Malachi) for approximately 400 years. If Mary's song celebrated a Messiah who would lift the lowly, Zechariah's song celebrates a Messiah who will bring Israel's salvation.

The word 'salvation' is repeated three times – but salvation from what? Zechariah longs for political protection: 'salvation from our enemies and from the hand of all who hate us' (v. 71), so that God's people could 'serve him without fear' (v. 74). At heart, Zechariah is a priest, and like the psalmists before him, he longs to minister in the temple. Although the Roman empire gave special dispensation at this point to the Jews to worship, having precarious permission is not the same as freedom. His desire to serve God without fear is a poignant one even today, where so many believers in the world cannot worship in freedom and risk their life every time they go to church.

However, if we just interpret this song as a desire for political freedom, we do Zechariah a disservice. Zechariah eagerly anticipates a spiritual rescue: 'the knowledge of salvation through the forgiveness of their sins' (v. 77). The enemies of God in Luke's gospel are not Israel's historical or political enemies, but Satan, the powers of evil – and sin. It is spiritual warfare that Jesus is interested in.

What does salvation from sin look like? Sheila Akomiah-Conteh told me that one of the Ghanaian titles for God is 'oye adie yie' in the Twi or Akan language (pronounced 'oi-ya day-ee'). This translates roughly as 'He does things well'. That same phrase, however, is also associated with mobile tailors who visit village by village. On the day they arrive, they call out repeatedly to advertise their services, 'oye adie yie', which in this context means 'He fixes well', and the residents know the fixer is here. That day, no matter what else is on your agenda, you all run and get all your old clothes because today is the day that everything can be mended. This is what Zechariah is saying: the day has come when God will visit. The Fixer is here.

In Ghana, there is no shame in everyone seeing your ripped or frayed clothes, because everyone else in the village is waiting in line with theirs.

'You are not alone in your brokenness,' Sheila explains with quiet tenderness. 'We are all tattered.'

She continues: 'I see God like that tailor. He goes for the broken, the tattered, the things we don't want to see in public. That is his job – to fix those broken things to make them good again.'[15]

In Jesus' time, looking back at the prophets, many imagined the Messiah coming to take his place on an earthly throne first, and the forgiveness of sins coming afterwards. In fact, it was the other way round. However great our need for worldly freedom (and that is significant), having spiritual freedom to freely access God, our sins forgiven, our ripped lives lovingly mended, is even more important. We can long for the one while praising God for the other.

## Reflect

- What do you think about the metaphor of God as tailor or seamstress?
- What does the word 'salvation' mean to you?
- What song of salvation has God given you to sing?

## Pray

*Lord, be with us this day,*
*within us to purify us;*
*above us to draw us up;*
*beneath us to sustain us;*
*before us to lead us;*
*behind us to restrain us;*
*around us to protect us.*
St Patrick, c. 389–461

## Sing

'Come, thou long expected Jesus' (Charles Wesley, 1707–88, music 'Hyfrydol' by Rowland Prichard, 1811–87).

# 17 December

## Those living in shadow are given mercy

**'Because of the tender mercy of our God,**
**by which the rising sun will come to us from heaven**
**to shine on those living in darkness**
**and in the shadow of death,**
**to guide our feet into the path of peace.'**
LUKE 1:78–79

When Gail was a child, she developed a profound fear of death. Her head teacher died suddenly, then her beloved Sunday school teacher, both in their 40s, and it seemed like anyone could drop dead without warning. At night-time, her fears became entwined with church imagery. In the early hours of the morning, she would wake in terror that the Angel of Death would come for her, then crawl each night into her mother's bed. At least, she reasoned, if the Angel of Death came, he would scoop both of them up together and she wouldn't be alone.

The Bible is honest about the horror of death. The apostle Paul called it 'the last enemy to be destroyed' (1 Corinthians 15:26). Death is not natural; it was not there in the perfection of Eden and it will be absent from heaven. Jesus will destroy the destroyer.

In the meantime, the tendrils of death's terror surround us. Yet we are not alone: God promises to accompany us through 'the valley of the shadow of death' (Psalm 23:4, KJV). Isaiah foretold of a great light

(Isaiah 9:1–2), and now Zechariah announces that that light is coming, through Jesus' arrival, to 'shine on those living in darkness', so we can walk a 'path of peace' (v. 79).

Gail's anxiety around death lasted for many years, but when she returned to faith as an adult, that fear gradually began to be replaced by God-given peace. God was with her in the shadows. This is not to say that she was utterly unafraid of death, but God relieved her extreme anxiety.

The word 'mercy' is mentioned eight times in Luke's gospel, and four of those uses are in this first chapter. Mary praises God for showing mercy 'to those who fear him' (v. 50), Zechariah thanked God for 'mercy to our ancestors' (v. 72), and his neighbours acknowledged God's 'mercy' to Elizabeth when she safely gave birth to a son (v. 58). In this final part of Zechariah's blessing, he looks to God's 'tender mercy' (v. 78), that beautiful phrase that speaks of God's care of and compassion for us. For Luke, Jesus' birth is God's mercy.

What exactly is mercy? Showing mercy is the three-stage process of: 1) seeing someone in need or suffering; 2) feeling compassion for them; and 3) acting to give them relief. This is well-illustrated in Jesus' famous parable of a good Samaritan who saw a man beaten and lying on the side of the road (Luke 10:25–37). Though others passed by the man, the Samaritan 'saw him, he took pity on him... and took care of him' (vv. 33–34). The Samaritan is then described as, 'The one who had mercy on him' (v. 37). This is what God does for us: God sees us in our needs, our weakness, our stuck-ness, and our fears; God has compassion upon us; and then God acts to take care of us.

God has given us the gift of Mercy, capital M, via Jesus' death and resurrection that have destroyed the power of death itself. Additionally, though, in smaller ways, God's 'mercies never come to an end; they are new every morning' (Lamentations 3:22–23, RSV). God's compassionate mercy is a gift we can unwrap every day; it never runs out.

## Reflect

- What do you think of the three-part definition of mercy?
- How have you experienced God's mercies over the years?
- What song of mercy/mercies has God given you to sing?
- What songs of light in the darkness has God given you?

## Pray

*O God,*
*you see me,*
*in the shadows, in the mud, in the fog,*
*in my suffering and despair,*
*my anxiety and fears.*

*You feel my pain*
*and you are moved by it.*

*Please act now, once again,*
*show me mercy, O Lord,*
*take care of me,*
*and may your light dawn upon me and never grow dim.*
*Amen.*

## Sing

'You never let go' (Matt Redman, 2006).

## 18 December

# The angels break their silence

**And there were shepherds living out in the fields near by, keeping watch over their flocks at night. An angel of the Lord appeared to them, and the glory of the Lord shone around them, and they were terrified. But the angel said to them, 'Do not be afraid. I bring you good news that will cause great joy for all the people. Today in the town of David a Saviour has been born to you; he is the Messiah, the Lord. This will be a sign to you: you will find a baby wrapped in cloths and lying in a manger.'**

**Suddenly a great company of the heavenly host appeared with the angel, praising God and saying,**

**'Glory to God in the highest heaven,**
**and on earth peace to those on whom his favour rests.'**

LUKE 2:8–14

For this final song of the series, we jump forward in time from Mary's pregnancy to the moment after the birth, when an angel appears to the shepherds. First comes the glory of God, as dazzling, terrifying light and weightiness (v. 9). Second comes 'great joy', because the Messiah has been born 'to you' (vv. 10–11), recalling Isaiah's proclamation that 'to us a child is born' (Isaiah 9:6). The third gift is God's peace, an ongoing state of harmony between God and people (v. 14).

Light, joy, peace, David's ancestry, and a child born: this is all imagery from Isaiah 9. The prophecy of the boy who will also be 'Mighty God' is now fulfilled.

But what most sticks with me is the behaviour of the angels. One angel arrives to deliver a message, which is God's usual pattern. Then 'suddenly' – unexpectedly – there are hundreds, perhaps thousands of angels. The phrase translated 'a great company of the heavenly host' sounds like they're sitting round for dinner, but it is military language, perhaps better translated as 'a multitude of the heavenly army', who are all 'praising God' (v. 13).

Their outburst reminds me of when my son was three, and we were preparing him to be a wedding guest for the first time. We explained the whole ceremony and told him there was a point where he also could join in. First, the minister will ask the married couple, 'Will you…' with all kinds of promises, and they will say, 'I will.' Then the minister will ask the friends and family to help them keep their promises. That's when we say together, 'We will.' My boy nodded and rehearsed the phrase, 'We will.'

The day came, the bride and groom faced each other at the front, and there was an attentive hush as the congregation stilled to hear their vows. The vicar asked the groom, 'Will you, Tom, take Lizzie to be your wife?' And as Tom stood there in all solemnity, considering his promise, one very loud, high-pitched voice from the congregation declared, 'We will!' The church fell apart laughing, the vicar asked Lizzie whether she wanted to consider my son's offer, and they had to begin the vows again.

My boy was so excited about what was going to happen that nothing could stop him from shouting out. I imagine the angels felt similarly. However long humans had been waiting for the Messiah, the company of heaven had longed for this day since the dawn of time. This good news was of cosmic importance, and the angels, after watching this scene silently and invisibly, burst into praise, glorifying God.

Today, of course, the earth groans, and humanity awaits Christ's return when our joy will be undiminished and our peace unlimited. It's all too easy to forget, as we plod along the highs and lows of this life, that there is even better to come. On that day, there will be angels again breaking their long silence with trumpets and songs of praise – and we, at last, will get to join in.

## Reflect

- What helps you refresh your excitement about Jesus?
- How does thinking of the cosmic, heavenly perspective help you as you consider the state of the world right now?
- What have your silences been, good and bad?
- What songs have you been given?

## Review

1. Elizabeth's song of wonder encouraged others.
2. Mary's song of joy celebrated God's kindness to her.
3. Mary's song of social justice called for revolution.
4. Zechariah's song of praise followed a time of personal silence.
5. Zechariah's song of salvation declared, 'The fixer is here.'
6. Zechariah's song of mercy comforted those in darkness.
7. The angels' song of excitement rejoiced in Jesus' coming.

Which of these songs do you most relate to?

## Pray

*Lord God, we praise you for Jesus' birth and long for his return. Glory to God in the highest.*

## Sing

'Light of the world' (Lauren Daigle, 2016).

4

# Giving up

# Introduction

As a child, Cara was enchanted by Christmas, and the anticipation of it was almost as good: the wreath-making, the marking of days, the tactile pleasure of opening an Advent calendar door with glitter on it. On Christmas Eve each year, she dressed as an angel for the local candlelit crib service, and when she returned home – gasp! – there were decorations everywhere and her parents had brought in a fully-dressed Christmas tree. Her skin tingled in wonder.

By the time Cara was an adult, the miracle of Christ's birth, the gift of knowing God, the magic of Christmas, and the joy of childhood were all tied up together, salvation and wonder, glitter and liturgy. When her husband proposed, Cara's first topic of discussion for married life was not children or money but how they would celebrate Christmas.

## Losing Christmas

Fast forward to another Christmas Day, when Cara's own daughter, Felicity, was merely days old. The midwife popped round and paled; Felicity was so dehydrated that she was in danger of having a stroke, and Cara had had no idea that anything was wrong. Felicity was rushed to hospital. Instead of enjoying a turkey dinner, Cara watched over her baby girl hooked up to a drip, praying for her survival. The spectre of trauma overshadowed them both every subsequent year.

On Felicity's fourth Christmas, Cara was awakened by her daughter's howling. She rushed to her room. Felicity was in significant distress, refusing to come down and screaming, 'I don't want presents! I don't want presents!' Felicity eventually only emerged on the promise that it would be a normal day, so Cara cleared the kitchen of all cheer, wondering if they would have to cancel Christmas altogether. Even

Cara's younger child, picking up on Felicity's anxiety, became afraid of the presents. It was a surreal moment when Cara considered that chasing her toddling son around the house while he ran away from his gifts really wasn't the best way to introduce someone to Christmas.

What Cara later realised was that Felicity was autistic, and the uncertainty, noise, and social expectations involved in Christmas Day were far beyond her coping threshold. Cara had been thrilled to share her family's Advent traditions, plus more of her own, to build up the buzz for Christmas. But when a child has a dysregulated nervous system, anticipation and fear are experienced as the same thing. What Cara interpreted as excitement was Felicity's increasing terror.

That Christmas, all jollity muted, Cara was devastated, mainly because she had inadvertently terrorised her daughter. She was also afraid. It felt like standing on the edge of a black hole, staring into the depths of uncertainty, frightened of tipping over into a future where everything would have to change.

Then and there, Cara lost Christmas and all its interconnected strands – baby Jesus, joy and peace, tradition and ritual, expectations of motherhood, hope for the future. All these were boxed up at the end of the season and stored in a quiet, unseen place in Cara's heart.

From then, they still marked Christmas Day, carefully navigating it to meet both children's needs, but it had become a thing to dread. All was not calm, but chaotic instead. Still a deeply seasonal person, Cara tried to become an Easter fan, as death and resurrection were themes she resonated with at that time. But something still felt lacking.

## Gaining Christ

Over the years, something shifted. Cara gave up Christmas in the sense of giving upwards, surrendering it to God. Some Christmas traditions were sacrificed, most were adapted, and as Felicity grew older her tolerance for Christmas expanded. Because Cara knew of other families whose children couldn't manage Christmas Day at all, she counted herself lucky. She created new traditions, personalised for her children.

Cara gradually discovered that the Christmas elements she had found so much joy in were truly only symbols. The real thing was still miraculous. Having given up Christmas, she received a sharpened appreciation of the incarnation. Stripped of all its accoutrements, the simple truth of God entering our world was all the more glorious.

When I ask what Christmas means to her now, her eyes light up.

'The incarnation is utterly extraordinary!' she says, then pauses. 'Christmas is more deeply important to me now than when it was important to me just because I loved Christmas.'

Cara gave up Christmas and rediscovered Christ.

Sometimes, as Christians, we are called to give up something bad, perhaps quitting a damaging habit or an ambition that won't ultimately serve us. Sometimes we are called to sacrifice something good. We might give up individual goals for the sake of family considerations or financial luxuries for others in need. This takes real discernment, however; depriving ourselves because we don't feel worthy of good things is very different from God's clear and specific prompting. When God calls us to give something up, as we see with Joseph and the Magi, it is not to make us miserable but lead us to something greater.

Other times, when we feel powerless or anxious, we are called to 'give upwards', towards heaven, placing everything into God's hands. Instead of endless internal struggle, we bring our wrestling to God in prayer – and find peace.

Shops and relentless adverts associate Christmas with gain. Yet for so many, celebrating Christmas is itself a sacrifice. Others have had something precious taken from them and are grieving. Others find

Christmas so difficult they give up all expectations and traditions, adapting and adjusting, like Cara.

Among the wreckage of disappointment and loss, there are often still gems of goodness to discover, if we look hard enough. If Christmas is difficult for you, I invite you to find yourself in the following passages, and to know God alongside you in it all. Joseph gave up his rights, Mary was deprived of choice surrounding her labour, shepherds and magi temporarily gave up precious things, and Jesus left heaven behind. The very first Christmas involved immense sacrifice and surrender, and still more glorious reward. Even if we lose Christmas, may we always find Christ.

# 19 December

## Joseph gives up his right to divorce

**This is how the birth of Jesus the Messiah came about: his mother Mary was pledged to be married to Joseph, but before they came together, she was found to be pregnant through the Holy Spirit. Because Joseph her husband was faithful to the law, and yet did not want to expose her to public disgrace, he had in mind to divorce her quietly.**

**But after he had considered this, an angel of the Lord appeared to him in a dream and said, 'Joseph son of David, do not be afraid to take Mary home as your wife, because what is conceived in her is from the Holy Spirit.'**

MATTHEW 1:18–20

I have always loved the musical *Les Misérables*, so when I was 18, I read the original novel, a two-volume doorstopper of over 1,000 pages. The opening scene with the convict Valjean stealing from a bishop is over within five minutes of the musical, so I was dismayed to have read 40 densely written pages in tiny font and still not have met Valjean. Instead, I'd endured a full audit of all the bishop's belongings, which is how I know that he sat on straw chairs, had an old sideboard for an altar, and lay on an iron hospital bed.

The bishop allowed himself one small luxury: a set of silver dinner plates. As we later learn, tin smells and iron affects taste, so he would not have enjoyed his food without the silver. He had also inherited two candlesticks, which he brought out to honour guests.

The bishop offered Valjean hospitality when everyone else rejected him, treating him like a respected guest. But Valjean betrayed his kindness by stealing the silver plates. When Valjean is caught, he faces the dreaded return to imprisonment. However, the bishop lies to the police, so that Valjean is released. This is a majestically generous and merciful act in itself. But there is more to come, and those pages of description finally pay off: the bishop also gives Valjean his precious silver plates and those beautiful candlesticks.

This always bothered me. The bishop had already gone above and beyond – and now he's supposed to give up his nice dinners? It seemed unfair.

Perhaps it was Joseph's story that inspired Victor Hugo for this particular plot. We have reached the part in the story when Mary has left Elizabeth's house, returning to Nazareth, approximately three months pregnant, her belly probably announcing the scandal to the whole village before she could tell Joseph.

Remember that in this honour–shame culture, Joseph wasn't just dealing with Mary's presumed infidelity; this was a disgrace that would make him a laughing stock to his community and besmirch his whole family. A challenge had been made to his honour, and the only way of reclaiming it would be to shame Mary publicly. Having her stoned to death may have been extreme but permissible. He may have even understood it as a religious obligation: the attempted stoning of the woman caught in adultery reveals that this practice still happened in Jesus' day (John 8:1–11). That was his right.

By quietly divorcing her (v. 19), Joseph would already be going above and beyond any standards of mercy at great cost to himself. Who could ask for more from him?

God did. The angel of the Lord told Joseph to take Mary immediately as his wife and accept that the conception was the work of the Holy Spirit. When Joseph obeyed the angel against his better judgement, he unknowingly gained a far greater honour than the one he sacrificed: the adopted father of God-the-Son himself.

This is the great challenge of the Christian call. Not always, but sometimes, even when we're congratulating ourselves for doing far more than the average Christian, God's Spirit stirs our heart in a particular way and says, 'You need to give more.' It's not fair, it's even not reasonable. Yet occasionally God calls us to an extra fast for the sake of someone else's feast.

## Reflect

- What inspires you about Joseph's actions?
- What does the angel's visit to Joseph, not just Mary, tell you about God?

## Pray

*Lord Jesus,*
*make us as obedient, generous and faithful as Joseph,*
*and grant us the discernment to know when you are calling us*
*to give more –*
*irrationally more –*
*knowing that you give abundantly, exuberantly, beyond all reason*
*to us.*
*Amen.*

# 20 December

## Joseph gives up his naming privileges

**'She will give birth to a son, and you are to give him the name Jesus, because he will save his people from their sins'…**

**When Joseph woke up, he did what the angel of the Lord had commanded him and took Mary home as his wife. But he did not consummate their marriage until she gave birth to a son. And he gave him the name Jesus.**

MATTHEW 1:21, 24–25

It is a great privilege to choose a name for a child. In the Hebrew Bible, usually it was the mothers who named their children. Scholars say that by Jesus' day it was the right of the father to name the child, typically naming a son after his paternal grandfather. However, one look at Joseph's genealogy indicates that wasn't a pattern Joseph's family had followed.

Joseph knew from the angel that Mary had not been unfaithful to him. Still, I wonder, why did God not give Joseph the grace of at least naming the child, so he could feel included?

One reason was because God choosing the name meant this child was special. Jesus' name would explain his mission to the world: to 'save people from their sins' (v. 21), just as Zechariah had also prophesied (Luke 1:77). Jesus, 'Yeshua' in Arabic and 'Joshua' in our Bibles, means roughly, 'The Lord saves'.

When I visited Zimbabwe, I met a couple who had named their first-born using similar principles. Because they were grateful to God, they christened their daughter, 'Tatenda', which is 'Thank you' in Shona. As British visitors with very limited Shona, we at least had learned to thank our hosts, and every time we did, the little toddler would run up to us with eyes of expectation because we had said her name.

The first Joshua, Moses' spiritual successor, led God's people out of the wilderness and into the promised land. This second Joshua would lead all peoples out of sin and death into eternal life. Like the little girl named 'Thank you', every time someone called for Jesus throughout his life, they would simultaneously be proclaiming, 'The Lord saves!'

Consider this, too: angels told Joseph and Mary separately that the child should be named Jesus (Matthew 1:21; Luke 1:31). Whenever they broached the subject of names, Mary and Joseph could both say simultaneously, 'His name will be Jesus', and know for sure that God had visited the other. This was a kindness of God for their mutual reassurance.

Finally, though I don't want to push too hard with this metaphor, it's interesting to compare Jesus to a late-adopted child. Jesus' real family of origin, if you consider his pre-existence, was not really Mary but God the Father and Holy Spirit (John 1:1–3). It makes sense that they chose his earthly name. Jesus was not a typical adopted child, because he was divine, the creator of the world, and born for a very specific purpose. Also, the pre-existent Jesus chose to leave home, whereas adoptive children today are often taken from their birth parents for complex reasons of safety or tragedy. Yet Jesus' experience of feeling torn between two families as he grew up, loving his parents yet craving contact with his family of origin, is familiar to many adopted children.

Although we don't often consider God's perspective in this, the three members of God the Trinity would have carried a grief of separation, of sorts, while Jesus was incarnate. Yet they also rejoiced in fulfilling their plan to save humanity.

Mary and Joseph also struggled with this (for example, when twelve-year-old Jesus stayed behind in his 'Father's house') yet were grateful to parent the Messiah (Luke 2:49). In adoption, as in life, there is often sacrifice all around, accompanied by grief, joy, and gratitude, all wrapped up together. And God the Holy Trinity has experienced it all.

## Reflect

- What do you find helpful about the metaphor of adoption in Jesus' family? What are its limitations?
- Where in your life have you sacrificed, only to be profoundly grateful for doing so?
- If you were to choose a spiritual name for yourself, what would it be?

## Pray

Meditate on Jesus' name, using the following verses.

> Our God is a God who saves;
>     from the Sovereign Lord comes escape from death.
> PSALM 68:20

> Lord, you are the God who saves me;
>     day and night I cry out to you.
> PSALM 88:1

> 'The Lord your God is with you,
>     the Mighty Warrior who saves.
> He will take great delight in you;
>     in his love he will no longer rebuke you,
>     but will rejoice over you with singing.'
> ZEPHANIAH 3:17

# 21 December

## Jesus gave up heaven for a manger

**So Joseph also went up from the town of Nazareth in Galilee to Judea, to Bethlehem the town of David, because he belonged to the house and line of David. He went there to register with Mary, who was pledged to be married to him and was expecting a child. While they were there, the time came for the baby to be born, and she gave birth to her firstborn, a son. She wrapped him in cloths and placed him in a manger, because there was no guest room available for them.**

LUKE 2:4–7

Of course, Mary should have given birth in the comfort of her own home in Nazareth, surrounded by her female family members while Joseph waited outside to preserve his wife's modesty.

Unfortunately, that pesky Caesar Augustus wanted more tax, so Jesus was born in Bethlehem instead, fulfilling Micah's prophecy (Luke 2:1–3; Micah 5:2).

The only three details of Jesus' arrival are as follows: first, Mary swaddled Jesus; second, Jesus was laid in a feeding trough because, third, 'There was not for them a place in the *kataluma*' (v. 7, literally translated).

What is a *kataluma*? For centuries, translators guessed it meant 'inn'.[16] It's still possible there existed a friendly innkeeper with a stable, beloved of all children's nativities, but it's highly improbable that a village like

Bethlehem (population c. 300–1,000) could keep an inn in business. More likely, *kataluma* meant a 'guest room' on the mezzanine floor of someone's home.

Recent scholarship has fleshed out the skeletal details as follows: a guest room was perhaps too small to give birth in, so Mary gave birth in the larger lower space in a typical house, where people cooked and domestic animals stayed on cold nights. The hospitality culture of first-century Israel meant no self-respecting Jew would turn away guests, let alone one who could recite the same names as you on their family tree and another who was heavily pregnant. Mary and Joseph were welcomed into a relative's house joyfully full to the gunwales. Therefore, Jesus was born in poverty but surrounded by love.[17]

Both possible scenarios add an air of cosiness and harmony to the birth, but poverty is not romantic, and something in Luke's telling feels – off. Picture me as a detective, interrogating the evidence.

Who would prioritise a guest room for anyone other than a labouring woman, even if it was a little smaller? If giving birth in the downstairs space was a natural choice, why does Luke emphasise there was no room in the guest room, as though something were amiss? If the guest room was too small for Mary to deliver there, how was it big enough to hold all the men who couldn't be on the lower floor to protect Mary's modesty?

Assuming the Bethlehem relatives' hospitality, was an animal trough really the best substitute they had for a baby's cot? Was Mary not given a bed where Jesus could co-sleep? Why was the manger singled out as a special 'sign' for which the shepherds searched (Luke 2:12)?

Although it was typical for a newborn to be swaddled, why did Mary have to do it herself instead of resting while womenfolk helped? If many relatives were there, why do the shepherds only mention finding Mary, Joseph, and the baby together (Luke 2:16)? Luke drew parallels between Elizabeth and Mary, so why would he omit any mention of the extended family, whereas 'neighbours and relatives' are mentioned twice in Elizabeth's birth account (Luke 1:58, 65)?

The case for Jesus being born among family is based on the honour–shame culture which valued hospitality. No devout Jew would refuse a guest in need.

Except.

Except you might risk the shame of turning guests away if there were a greater shame in welcoming people into your home who have disgraced the family name. Though no one knows for sure, my theory as to why 'there was not *for them* a place in the *kataluma*' anywhere in Bethlehem is that Jesus' own relatives refused to welcome a supposedly adulterous woman. The punishment for adultery was death by stoning by the whole community (John 8:1–11; Deuteronomy 22:20–21). Because of Joseph's marriage to Mary, few people later in Jesus' life would know Joseph had not fathered him – but his family would surely know.

We don't know where Jesus was born, only where he was not born (the *kataluma*), and as early as c. AD150 Justin Martyr claimed Jesus' birthplace was a cave.[18] These caves were built into the rock in Bethlehem, often attached to houses and used for holding animals. Logically, if it were warm enough for sheep to be out in the field that night with shepherds (Luke 2:8), the cave would be unoccupied. This might explain how the shepherds found them so quickly with the manger. Perhaps this was a compromise that Joseph's relatives settled upon: concession with condemnation.

Jesus was definitely born into poverty, and perhaps disgrace and rejection, too. What a way to enter the planet you created – laid in a trough that sheep's tongues have licked. Luke wants us to be shocked. In birth, Jesus chose to identify with the poor, shaming anyone who has 'no room' for others in need. Where is our outrage?

## Reflect

- How do you fill in the story left by the skeleton details of the manger and 'no room'? Which explanation sounds most plausible for you?
- Which scenario of Jesus' birth circumstances do you personally *wish* it had been? Why is this?
- In our Christian churches, what unspoken exceptions are there in practice to the principle that 'everyone is welcome'?
- What part might you play in offering radical hospitality?

## Pray

- Today, whenever you see a closed door, pray for people not typically welcomed by society and individuals known to you who feel excluded.
- Whenever you see an open door, thank God for welcoming you and pray for opportunities for radical hospitality.

## 22 December

# The shepherds risk losing their sheep

**When the angels had left them and gone into heaven, the shepherds said to one another, 'Let's go to Bethlehem and see this thing that has happened, which the Lord has told us about.'**

**So they hurried off and found Mary and Joseph, and the baby, who was lying in the manger. When they had seen him, they spread the word concerning what had been told them about this child, and all who heard it were amazed at what the shepherds said to them. But Mary treasured up all these things and pondered them in her heart. The shepherds returned, glorifying and praising God for all the things they had heard and seen, which were just as they had been told.**

LUKE 2:15–20

The angels gave the shepherds treasure-hunt instructions to find the baby who would be the 'Saviour', and, without a second thought, 'they hurried off' (v. 16). Luke uses the same phrase in the Greek when Mary hurries to Elizabeth's house (Luke 1:39). A shepherd's one task is to guard their sheep, and Jesus' later parables indicate the dangers to a flock, including wolves and thieves (John 10). Yet those same shepherds abandoned their post to find Jesus. In an instant, their priorities had shifted. Thus, the first people to visit the Shepherd promised by Micah would be shepherds themselves.

When the angels called them to look for Jesus, the shepherds were also being called to trust God to protect the sheep in their absence. It can be surprisingly hard to trust God like this.

Gail had a tough childhood in many ways. Her father was largely absent and her mother had a disability, so Gail could never be fully sure of a steady income in her family. From this, she learned at a relatively young age that she was on her own and had to look after herself. She left behind her Sunday School faith in God and made her own way in the world.

In her 20s, she and her husband emigrated from southern Africa to Britain, ready for a fresh start. Unfortunately, their bank refused to believe they had left the country and froze their accounts. Then, all the furniture and luggage they'd sent on ahead by ship were lost. With little more than a suitcase full of summer clothes, they turned up at a friend's house in London, just as the weather was turning colder, and begged to stay with them.

For the first time in years, with nowhere else to turn, Gail prayed. 'If you are there, God,' she said, 'I need a job, a car, and a place to stay.'

The next day, she found a dream apartment for rent, only to discover she was the 25th person who had requested it. Despite this, the agent took pity on her. That apartment became her haven for the next few years. Then a distant relative, out of the blue, gifted them a car. When Gail turned up at an employment agency, they promptly offered her a job working for them. Although she didn't get paid until the end of the month, in that first week Gail won a Marks and Spencer's voucher so sizeable that she could buy good winter coats for them both. The next week she won a food voucher that fed them for a month.

Faced with this level of clearly answered prayer in such a short timeframe, Gail surrendered. All her life, she had provided for herself yet carried the constant fear of losing everything. But at that crucial time, God turned up for her as a loving parent and provider. Not only did she become a Christian, but she let go of that huge weight of always having to look out for herself.

This doesn't mean that God grants every request. Certainly, Gail's life was not free of difficulty after that point, but trusting God was liberating for her. If you feel crushed by the weight of having to rely only on yourself, I wonder if perhaps the shepherds can inspire you to risk taking a break, just for a moment, and dare to trust a little more in the Provider and Shepherd who takes care of the sheep.

## Reflect

- How easily do you trust God to provide for you? Why do you think that is?

## Pray

*O Lord, my Shepherd,*
*be my protection, and guard me from the devouring wolves;*
*be my provider, and grant to me a feast of enough;*
*be my peace, and lead me to the quiet streams.*
*Amen.*

# 23 December

## The Magi leave their home

**After Jesus was born in Bethlehem in Judea, during the time of King Herod, Magi from the east came to Jerusalem and asked, 'Where is the one who has been born king of the Jews? We saw his star when it rose and have come to worship him'...**

**'In Bethlehem in Judea,' they replied, 'for this is what the prophet has written...'**

**After they had heard the king, they went on their way, and the star they had seen when it rose went ahead of them until it stopped over the place where the child was.**

MATTHEW 2:1–2, 5, 9

Manny Mvula grew up in a rural village in Zambia, southern Africa, and was raised as a Christian. As a child, he had a vivid dream in which God told him: 'The only way to save you is for you to follow the northern star.'

Time passed and his faith faded. His hobby of observing nature in his youth led to a career as a safari guide. While employed by a British ecologist, he was literally dodging the poachers' bullets and engaging in self-destructive, risk-taking behaviours. He felt an emptiness, like something was missing.

One time, he was driving in the wild and spotted something out of the corner in his eye: an animal hiding behind a bush. Upon closer examination, he found the species to be human: a researcher named Cheryl who was desperately hoping that the elephants all around her wouldn't charge. She was grateful for his rescue.

Sometime later, Manny had an extraordinary opportunity: some safari clients were so impressed by his encyclopaedic knowledge of ecology that they offered to cover all his costs to study at The University of Manchester for an MA in conservation. With joy and trepidation, Manny travelled to Britain for his dream qualification, following that northern star. There, a second mini-miracle occurred: Cheryl got back in touch; they fell in love and were married. Still, something felt missing.

The Magi (from which we get our word 'magic') were likely a group of astrologers from Persia or Babylon. They associated certain stars with the death or birth of rulers.[19]

The faith of the Magi was extraordinary: from the extra brightness of one celestial object, they not only calculated the future birth of a king (of a people who did not share their faith) but left everything to find him. These rich academics didn't stay in a library but pursued the implications of their discovery. Ironically, the law of Moses forbade God's people from using 'divination', including astrology, to predict future events, urging them to listen to prophets instead (Deuteronomy 18:9–15). Yet here God spoke to foreigners through their own religion and culture.

Contrary to the nativity plays, though, the star did not initially lead them all the way to Bethlehem, just to Israel. There, apparently, the star disappeared. So, the Magi searched for the new king of the Jews in Israel's capital, Jerusalem. Unfortunately, they encountered Herod. Herod knew so little of the scriptures himself that he had to consult religious scholars, who informed the Magi of Micah's prophecy about Bethlehem, the Messiah's birthplace (Micah 5:2). After this conversation, the star reappeared and seemingly moved, leading them to Bethlehem, five miles south of Jerusalem (v. 9).

It is a two-stage process. The Magi stepped out in faith, based on the incomplete information they had, and arrived at the wrong place to meet the wrong king. Only after that did God lead them to their true destination. They had to go to Jerusalem first to reach Bethlehem.

Let us return to Manny, for his second stage. Cheryl wanted to go to a local church course exploring Christianity, mainly so she could disprove it all as an atheist. By the end of the course, both she and Manny had become Christians. When Manny recounts his story, his face radiates joy. 'Before, my vision was in black and white; now it is in colour,' he explains. 'I had to travel across the miles so I could meet Jesus, and that has completely transformed how I am.'

God led Manny by a northern star to his Jerusalem, in order that he would reach Bethlehem and find Jesus there. Often, I've discovered, this is the way that God guides. You don't have a clear idea of what is coming next, but you have that restless feeling that something is missing, and you need to step out in faith or leave what is comfortable. You arrive at a place that still doesn't feel quite right, questioning God's leading, only to be given further direction, perhaps from other people, once you're there.

Trying to discern God's guidance is hard, yet we who love Jesus also have the reassurance that he will be with us wherever we go.

## Reflect

- When have you experienced God's 'two-part' guidance? When have you left something without knowing what to go on to?
- To what extent have you lost your focus on Jesus and need to be guided back?

## Pray

*Lord, I cannot see the road ahead, but you can. I look to you; please guide me to the next right thing, and may I know your presence with me all the way. Amen.*

# 24 December

## Wise people give up precious gifts

**When they saw the star, they were overjoyed. On coming to the house, they saw the child with his mother Mary, and they bowed down and worshipped him. Then they opened their treasures and presented him with gifts of gold, frankincense and myrrh. And having been warned in a dream not to go back to Herod, they returned to their country by another route.**
MATTHEW 2:10–12

When I was a child, my hometown had a royal visitor: Diana, Princess of Wales. I was thrilled to meet a real princess, and my mum bought a bunch of flowers for me to give her as she passed. I stood outside in the cathedral precincts, seemingly for hours, in my scratchy coat, holding tightly to the cellophane-wrapped flowers, straining my head above the metal barrier. At last, she emerged with an entourage and walked along the passage, shaking hands and accepting gifts from children. My excitement grew.

She walked right past me. She never got my flowers. I was so devastated not to have given her my gift that I needed a chocolate bar for consolation. There is a photo commemorating my loss: pink glasses askew; face freshly moist from tears; me smiling bravely into the camera.

The Magi were similarly desperate to give their gifts to royalty. This was some time after the birth, though we don't know how long, when Mary and Joseph are apparently settled in Bethlehem, living in a house

(v. 11). It may be that the Bethlehemites warmed to the couple after the shepherds 'spread the word', amazing everyone there with the angels' confirmation that Jesus was 'the Messiah' (Luke 2:11, 17–18). If a relative claims divine intervention for their wife's conception, you may be sceptical, but if angels are also declaring the birth of the Messiah, you might change your mind.

In any case, the Magi are the first people to show honour to Jesus specifically. The shepherds praised *God* after seeing Jesus, but only the Magi are credited with venerating Jesus himself. The word translated 'worshipped' can mean paying homage to a king, bowing at his feet, but it can also mean worship of the divine. Perhaps Matthew is playing with the double-meaning, hinting that Jesus was also worthy of worship because he is God.

The Magi were obviously important people, and rich, too, yet they don't expect to be treated with special hospitality. Rather, they want to give up their treasures. They are not put off by humble surroundings; they just want to honour Jesus. Contrary to what we might expect, no excitement from Mary or Joseph is mentioned, but the givers of the gifts themselves are the ones feeling joy. In fact, when they spotted the star, the literal translation is approximately, 'they rejoiced exceedingly with a big joy' (v. 10).

The Magi inspire me. They came to Jesus without negotiating a political contract, without expectation of repayment or mention from this future king. They just wanted to honour him and were thrilled to do so.

So often, my relationship with God can end up feeling transactional, my prayer life consisting of a wish list presented to a heavenly Santa in the sleepy minutes before bedtime. I want to recover that joy of worshipping Jesus, honouring him for who he is. I want to give to Jesus my very best from whatever treasures I own, with that same excitement I had holding those flowers for Princess Diana. I encourage you to do the same, knowing that, unlike human royalty, Jesus will always accept – and delight in – whatever we bring to him.

## Reflect

- To what extent do you connect with the concept of rejoicing in worshipping Jesus?
- What do you have that you are giving to Jesus this coming year?

## Pray: part one

Spend time looking at or handling wrapped gifts today. Imagine giving gifts to Jesus, dedicating them to him. Choose from: your talents, your compassion, your work, your opportunities, your relationships, your resources, your treasures, etc.

> *Lord Jesus, I give you my… Please help me to glorify you through it/them. Amen.*

## Sing

'Take my life, and let it be' (Francis Ridley Havergal, 1836–79, music Nottingham, Mozart)

## Pray: part two

> *Lord Jesus, I give you my… [adoration, joy, worship, etc.] You are worthy of all praise. Amen.*

## Sing

'O come all ye faithful' (attributed to John Francis Wade, 1711–86, music Adeste Fidelis) as a worship song, with its invitation along with the Magi, 'O come, let us adore him'.

# 25 December

## We are given Immanuel

**All this took place to fulfil what the Lord had said through the prophet: 'The virgin will conceive and give birth to a son, and they will call him Immanuel' (which means 'God with us').**
MATTHEW 1:22–23

It is Christmas Day, and I am seven. The stockings lie heavy on the duvet, crammed with goodies, and I can hear my sister already ripping into her presents on the bottom bunk, paper strewn across the floor. It is finally here, this day of magic, and God is for me, and all is right with the world.

*

Helen lies in a hospital bed on Christmas Day with suspected meningitis or some other mysterious virus. Secluded in an isolation ward, the medics wander by, shrouded in masks, keeping their distance.

For a few precious minutes, her three small children were allowed to open presents at her bedside, and she revelled in the sweetness of the moment, then her husband waved goodbye and they departed. Only silence remains, and the passing of time.

A kind orderly brings her a tray of hospital food with a Christmas cracker on the side, then promptly exits. Helen looks at it. What is the point of a Christmas cracker when there is no one to pull it with her?

*

In Isaiah's day, God's people did not want to think anything bad would happen to them, which made the prophet very unpopular when he predicted an invasion from Assyria (Isaiah 7:13–20). The residents of Judah were invested in denial. They used the phrase 'God is with us' like a talisman, and young mothers named their children accordingly (Isaiah 7:14). 'Nothing bad will happen to our nation,' they proclaimed, 'because God will protect us from every evil. God is with us, so we will always be victorious. God is on our side no matter what.'

This is so often what I want from God. I want to be cosy in my duvet, protected from the world's evils. I want 'God is with me' to mean 'only good things will happen to me'. It's what I desire for my loved ones, and for you, my dear reader, and it is entirely understandable.

Unfortunately, though, things don't always go to plan. We are left lonely or bewildered. If we understand 'God with us' to be only 'good things happen, always', then we will be devastated on the day of disaster. This side of heaven, sorrow and celebration run on parallel tracks.

This is why we need Matthew, who sees in Isaiah's initial prophecy a greater reality to come. One day there would be a supernatural virgin birth, and the child called Jesus, 'God saves', would also be known as Immanuel, 'God with us'. Jesus was God with us, not metaphorically, but literally – entering humanity, born with muscle, blood, and skin.

For Helen, 'Immanuel' has become a statement of faith to lean upon.

'When faced with what often feels like weighty evidence to the contrary, God is in fact here,' she said. 'The creator of the universe, who said from the outset it's not good for us to be alone, gave himself – and gives himself daily – to his creation, so that we never are.'

God is not only above us but alongside us. Jesus' cross and resurrection is our hope for the future: eternal life in technicolour, with no more sorrow, sickness, or solitude. Jesus' incarnation is our comfort in the present. Jesus, Immanuel, says to us, 'I'm right here with you; I understand, and I will help you.'

Whatever other gifts we get from God: honour, favour, blessings, joy, hope, faith – they pale in comparison to the gift of Jesus himself, red and covered in vernix, lying in the manger.

## A poem for reflection

**Immanuel**

*Shepherds left their fields*
*and risked their flocks*
*to be with you.*

*You left heaven*
*to be with me.*

*Magi marched for miles*
*and wandered long*
*to find a king.*

*You came further*
*to search for me.*

*Angels waited years*
*then sang their songs*
*to tell of you.*

*You sang louder*
*of love for me.*

## Pray

*Jesus, Immanuel,*
*be with me in my rejoicing.*

*Jesus, Immanuel,*
*be with me in my weeping.*

*Be with me when I lose my step,*
*be with me as I stare through mist,*
*be with me when my soul is crushed,*
*draw near to me, I pray.*

*Be with me when I see with hope,*
*be with me when life feels like gift,*
*be with me when I thrill with joy,*
*rejoice with me, I pray.*

*Jesus, Immanuel,*
*be with me, by my side.*

*Jesus, Immanuel,*
*walk with me throughout my life.*
*Amen.*

5

# Pierced hearts

# Introduction

Having endured a year's treatment for a melanoma, Debbie believed she had beaten cancer. But at the beginning of December, she was hospitalised for treatment complications. Her parents travelled to help look after the children (11 and 6), while her friends, Christian and Abby Norman, joined her husband Josh at the hospital. On 15 December, Debbie became extremely fatigued. Despite working in medicine all her life, she could no longer understand what the doctors were saying. At that point, Abby realised in her gut: my friend is dying.

That was Monday. On Tuesday, the doctors admitted they could do nothing more for her. The church jumped into action: church members raised $800 for a hospital bed within two hours and installed it in Debbie's lounge, making the space clean and Christmassy. Debbie's best friend, Laurie, pulled an all-nighter wrapping up all the family's presents.

On Wednesday, the kids left school early to celebrate Christmas at home with their mother. Wonderfully, Debbie had two lucid hours with her family around her before she began to lose consciousness. Later that day, while Josh lay beside her and sang hymns softly into her ear, she passed from this world into the next.

Debbie had shaped her whole life around loving God and others. Professionally, she was a senior nurse in stroke care, undertaking doctorate research in how to improve healthcare for underserved populations. She had worked in malaria prevention in Africa, met her husband when they were leaders on a camp for disabled children, and loved her church and neighbourhood community well. Alongside Josh, she raised their children with compassion and kindness.

She was 38. Her death, as with so many others who die young, feels brutally unfair.

On the day Josh realised his wife was dying, he went out to the hospital car park with Abby and Christian and screamed to the heavens. Then he shouted a swear word as loudly as he could.

He looked at his friends.

'That didn't even help.'

Abby gripped Josh in as tight a hug as she could, while Christian embraced them both from behind.

Abby's words poured out: 'I'm here, I'm right here. We're with you. We are not leaving. We're with you.'

On the Sunday after Debbie's death, Josh showed up at church, though no one expected him to. He came with authenticity, carrying his raw grief, as he lay down on a pew. Someone put a pillow under his head and laid a blanket on top. Abby sat beside him, holding his hand. His brother-in-law sat on the floor at the other side, holding Josh's face in both hands. Family and friends behind Josh gently placed their hands on him. The person behind Abby held her hand. Symbolically and literally, the church community supported those closest to Debbie.

When it was time for the Eucharist, Josh went up to receive bread and wine. He found that he couldn't wait like the rest of the congregants, so he lay prostrate at the step. When it was time to give the Communion elements to him, the pastor, Angie, turned off her microphone. She crouched and then also lay down, right where he was, descending to his level rather than expecting him to come up to hers. She fed him with bread and wine and prayer.

Abby Norman is also my friend, and she wrote a book about being honest with God: *You Can Talk to God Like That: The surprising power of lament to save your faith* (Broadleaf Books, 2021). Two days after that Sunday service, I rang Abby to check how she was doing and ask what she would say to others grieving.

'The first thing to say is that death is horrible,' Abby said, nursing her cup of coffee. 'We do this thing with grief where we gloss over it. It *is* that bad. All these beautiful things coming out of this – the church's generosity and the specialness of Debbie's final hours, everything wonderful birthed out of the grief – does not for a second placate any of the sadness of this. This is trash. This is absolute garbage.'

She paused.

'So I guess I would say, second, that hope is about telling the truth.'

Recently, Abby had written a Substack letter, in which she explained her thinking:

'Pretending that everything is fine will never lead to anything but continued brokenness. In fact, telling that truth is, I believe, the first steps to hope. Telling the truth is in and of itself a hopeful act...

'But the brokenness is only half of the truth... If we say that it is broken, we can then go about fixing it, healing it, finding a new and not broken way...

'In this season, this has become the work for me of Advent, simply remembering that God did not abandon us in the brokenness, God met us there.'[20]

I nodded.

'So,' I asked, 'What does Christmas mean to you in all this?'

'Well, our Saviour came into the world and was pierced,' Abby replied. 'If we're going to be the hands and feet of Jesus, we're going to get pierced. I don't think there are many promises, real promises, this side of heaven, besides "God with us".'

She sipped her coffee and looked thoughtful.

'Here's what I do know. When the worst happens, God grabs us, just like I grabbed Josh in that parking lot outside the hospital, holds us tightly, and says, "I'm not going anywhere. I'm here. I'm right here with you."'

From Boxing Day till New Year's Eve, when the post-Christmas slump hits, we approach the darkest themes of the Christmas story, the horrors that accompanied Jesus' birth. We encounter hatred and oppression, homelessness and terror, trauma and its long-term impact. On the Feast of the Holy Innocents (28 December) we look at what the Bible says to people grieving the death of a child. It's hard in many ways, but important. As Abby says, hope begins with telling the truth.

In all of this, the message is that Christ came not only to be human, but to walk through the darkest shadows of the human existence. Angie coming down to Josh's level, in his pain, so perfectly reflects the incarnation. Christ descended to our level rather than expecting us to reach his. He is right there with us.

Abby's experience, however, reminds me that we who are believers are called to be the 'body of Christ' on earth. If we don't have anyone supporting us in our sadness, we still have Christ with us in the present and the future hope of a world made right. But it strikes me that so often Jesus' ministry to us is mediated through other people. We cannot be the Messiah to every suffering person; it is too much. Like Josh's church, however, we can be a hand. If all of us do that, the grieving person will be enveloped in God's love through us.

If today your heart is pierced, please take this section as my hand in yours and God's embrace around you. God is with us.

## 26 December

# Herod is invited to give up power

**When King Herod heard this he was disturbed, and all Jerusalem with him. When he had called together all the people's chief priests and teachers of the law, he asked them where the Messiah was to be born. 'In Bethlehem in Judea,' they replied, 'for this is what the prophet has written:**

**'"But you, Bethlehem, in the land of Judah,**
**are by no means least among the rulers of Judah;**
**for out of you will come a ruler**
**who will shepherd my people Israel."'**

**Then Herod called the Magi secretly and found out from them the exact time the star had appeared. He sent them to Bethlehem and said, 'Go and search carefully for the child. As soon as you find him, report to me, so that I too may go and worship him.'**

MATTHEW 2:3–8

Imagine a scenario: you have been working faithfully in your field, trusting that one day your talent and hard work will be rewarded. Then someone new appears on the scene, and suddenly everyone is talking about them. How do you feel about this new person?

Perhaps you feel resentful, hostile, jealous, wary, or angry. Behind all these emotions, I would suggest one big one: fear – of being replaced or losing power, your hopes for the future dissolving.

This is how Herod the Great felt when he heard about Jesus' birth.

Allow me to briefly introduce you to this particular Herod. The Romans appointed him to keep Judea in order, so Herod primarily served Caesar Augustus, not the people. The Roman Senate appointed him as 'King of the Jews', but ironically, though scholars believe he was raised as a Jew, ancient historian Josephus described him as an 'Idumean' (the Roman term for descendants of Edom) and referred to him as a 'half-Jew'.[21]

On his way to power, he fought off Antigonus, a challenger who fancied Herod's position. Herod taxed the people brutally, but hoped to win their favour through his many impressive building projects, especially the new temple. Over time, though, his imposter syndrome developed into greater fear. In his later years, he killed his brother-in-law and two of his sons, concerned that the Romans might want a younger ruler. He was like Stalin – powerful yet paranoid, killing every potential rival before they could challenge him.

This explains quite why Herod was so disturbed – agitated, even – by the announcement of a new king, descended from David like a long-lost heir. We tend to believe it was inevitable that Herod would choose violence and revenge, but he could have gone another way: collaboration rather than competition. We know this because of an example in Israel's history: Jonathan, King Saul's son and heir to the Israelite throne.

Jonathan recognised that David, the up-and-coming warrior, was God's chosen king to replace Saul. In other words, David was coming to take his job. Rather than kill him or feel threatened, Jonathan became his best friend and did everything he could to protect David (1 Samuel 19—24, 31).

I've often wondered why God allowed the Magi to encounter Herod in Jerusalem instead of sending them directly to Bethlehem. Could God have wanted to extend to Herod an invitation to be a better person, to give up his paranoid hold on power and share it instead?

Herod's request to the Magi to report back the location of the child was likely a plot to kill Jesus, yet I wonder whether any part of Herod's heart considered honouring Jesus and respecting God. Did his conscience wrestle with this or was he already so hardened by his previous violence to secure his position?

God gave Herod a choice between letting go of his power, just a little, to share it with another, but Herod opted for violent tyranny instead. Nothing is inevitable: there is always a choice.

## Reflect

- In your life, where do you face choices between competition and collaboration?
- How does Herod's example guide your prayers as you think of similar dictators today?

## Breath Prayers

Repeat as needed.

**Breathe in:** *Lord, where paranoid leaders today wreak violence,*
**Breathe out:** *please plague their conscience and bring justice.*

**Breathe in and clench fists:** *Lord, where I am clinging too tightly to power,*
**Breathe out and open palms:** *may I release that to you.*

**Breathe in:** *Lord, where my frustration turns to thoughts of revenge,*
**Breathe out:** *may I leave the battle to you.*

## 27 December

# Joseph loses his home

**When they had gone, an angel of the Lord appeared to Joseph in a dream. 'Get up,' he said, 'take the child and his mother and escape to Egypt. Stay there until I tell you, for Herod is going to search for the child to kill him.'**

**So he got up, took the child and his mother during the night and left for Egypt, where he stayed until the death of Herod. And so was fulfilled what the Lord had said through the prophet: 'Out of Egypt I called my son.'**

MATTHEW 2:13–15

Pastor Barnabas leads his congregation in worship. Hundreds gather under a make-shift shelter of sticks and brushwood to shade themselves from the oppressive African sun. Around the church are hundreds of closely packed tents that have served as homes for the past five years. Four people sleep in an area less than the footprint of a double bed, and their roof is made of cardboard.

The charity Open Doors reports that Barnabas is one of approximately 16 million internally displaced Christians in sub-Saharan Africa, meaning they are like refugees in their own country. Mary and Joseph's experience of running for their lives is shared by so many today. It is not a fairytale but brutal reality.

Pastor Barnabas was working on his farm alongside his sister-in-law and brother when they heard rapid shooting. The militants came, shouting hatred against Christians, and attacked them brutally. Pastor

Barnabas suffered grave injury from the machete attack. His brother and sister-in-law were both killed. Whole communities fled for their lives.

Pastor Barnabas feels the responsibility towards his flock.

'I don't have anything to give them,' he says. 'I am displaced myself.'

What he can offer is spiritual encouragement.

'We only pray together and share the word of God. Our eyes are on him. Our hope is on him.'[22]

Being stepfather to the Messiah was no picnic. Joseph barely had time to get his head around marrying Mary and raising a child instead of divorcing her when he was summoned to Bethlehem for non-ideal birthing conditions. By the time the Magi reached the holy family by starlight, however, the holy family had settled down in a Bethlehem home (Matthew 2:11). Possibly Joseph and Mary were more accepted in their community because of the testimony of the shepherds. The Magi's visit could have been either weeks or up to two years after the birth.

Though moving to Bethlehem at short notice was disruptive, it couldn't compare to waking after a terrifying dream, alerting your shocked wife and crying child, packing as quickly and quietly as you can and embarking on a long journey in the darkness, your heart thumping so loudly in your chest that you fear others will hear it. They had no opportunity to say goodbye, no chance of explaining their disappearance to friends or family.

Herod was a terrifying enemy. He had all the resources and might of the Roman state and all the vindictiveness of a deranged dictator. All they could do was run and hope they would never be identified as the threat to Herod's throne. The journey to Egypt was approximately 240–300 miles, depending on what route they took and their destination. By donkey, that would have taken at least a month, longer if they walked. Would they have spent the Magi's gold on food and lodgings?

On Christmas cards, the holy family are portrayed as serene, the flight to Egypt shown as a gentle stroll. But in practice, the journey meant carrying a tired, hungry, possibly still-breastfeeding child on an arduous journey while they were exhausted to the bone and beside themselves with worry.

I find it striking that God didn't shield even Jesus from the terror of persecution or childhood trauma. God didn't stop Herod's free will but worked within the situation, through dreams, to minimise the damage.

From his earliest moments, Jesus identified with refugees, asylum seekers, and traumatised children growing up in poverty and insecure housing. Jesus didn't come as a Teflon-coated saviour, immune from the threats of life. He came to be 'God with us' for survivors of terror.

## Reflect

- How might Jesus' experience as a refugee influence our response to refugees?
- As you think through others' (or your) experience of insecurity and trauma, to what extent do you see God working quietly within the situation?

## Breath prayer

**Breathe in:** *Lord Jesus, who became a refugee,*
**Breathe out:** *bring refuge to people in need.*

**Breathe in:** *Lord Jesus, who fled from angry men,*
**Breathe out:** *protect me still and give me haven.*

# 28 December

## Rachel loses her children

**When Herod realised that he had been outwitted by the Magi, he was furious, and he gave orders to kill all the boys in Bethlehem and its vicinity who were two years old and under, in accordance with the time he had learned from the Magi. Then what was said through the prophet Jeremiah was fulfilled:**

**'A voice is heard in Ramah,**
**weeping and great mourning,**
**Rachel weeping for her children**
**and refusing to be comforted,**
**because they are no more.'**

MATTHEW 2:16–18

Georgie Tennant's worst Christmas came when she was 25 weeks pregnant and hadn't felt much movement from the baby. On 23 December she had a scan that revealed her baby's heartbeat had stopped. On 27 December she delivered her baby stillborn. It was a little girl, and Georgie named her Grace.

Her grief was immense. Among her sadness hovered deep disappointment and great anger. Georgie wrestled with questions of faith like never before, and at times she even considered giving up on God altogether.

Scholars estimate the number of infants killed in Bethlehem at 12–30, as Bethlehem had an estimated population of 300–1,000. The slaughter didn't make the headlines and wasn't recorded by Josephus (leading some historians to question whether it even happened). Matthew, however, marked this awful chapter out of respect for the heartbreak of the parents involved. Losing a child is terrible under any circumstances. Losing a child to violent murder, while watching on and screaming for mercy, powerless to save your child, is absolutely unbearable.

Matthew's quotation from Jeremiah is worth explaining. Rachel was the beloved second wife of Jacob, and in Israel's historic imagination stood as the nation's mother. She was also an icon of suffering, having died in childbirth with Benjamin. She was buried somewhere around Bethlehem (Genesis 35:16–20).

In Jeremiah's time, the nation's great tragedy was the exile. Hundreds, perhaps thousands, of citizens would have died of starvation or disease while the city was under siege (see 2 Kings 25). Of those who survived, the fittest and best were gathered in Ramah before being deported to Babylon (Jeremiah 40:1). Jeremiah's prophecy pictures the long-dead Rachel, weeping over the country, sharing their sorrow.

Despite the low numbers of people affected, Matthew links the Bethlehem infant deaths to the greatest tragedies in Israel's history: the Babylonian exile and Pharaoh's slaughter of Israelite babies (Matthew 2:15). Jeremiah's description of Rachel's grief, devastating in its simplicity, hits me in the gut: 'Rachel weeping for her children and refusing to be comforted, because they are no more.' (v. 18).

Herod's legacy will never be his building projects but his cold cruelty in killing those precious children. We have no easy answers to this tragedy, no clear comfort for those parents. Instead, Matthew's account howls with outrage, publicly and prophetically expressing sorrow upon sorrow, so that everyone may be a witness, and God may be the judge.

Sometimes no comfort can be found, at least not for a long while, because the loss is too devastating. Platitudes and positive spins are sucked into the all-consuming vacuum of deepest grief. In that most lonely of darknesses, where all hope and light seem to have disappeared, only honest lament will help you survive.

Georgie eventually made her way back to faith, reasoning it was better to endure grief with God holding her hand. She hoped for eventual healing, which came slowly and through hard emotional work.

For those of us witnessing loved ones mired in grief, especially traumatic grief, it is likely our words of consolation will fall short. However, we can yet mark their sorrow like Matthew, rather than denying it, and weep and lament alongside them, like Rachel. Our churches need to embrace the psalmist's wails of 'How long, O Lord?' and reclaim the ministry of communal lament. When God feels far from the bereaved, we can be, as Abby Norman says, the hands and feet of 'God with us'.

## Breath prayer

**Breathe in:** *Why, Lord – why? How can I endure this?*
**Breathe out:** *I send my howls of pain to the one who hears my prayer.*

**Breathe in:** *As I walk through the valley of the shadow of death*
**Breathe out:** *be my light, my comfort, and my guide.*

## Reflect

You may want to use the poem by Georgie Tennant on the following page as the basis of prayer.

## Christmas baby

*A Christmas baby –*
*not the kind we'd assume would arrive,*
*full of warmth, life, cuddles, joy,*
*but stillness; silence.*
*The cot, painfully empty.*
*Exiting the delivery suite*
*with no special delivery.*
*Empty, hurting, reeling,*
*wondering how this could ever be redeemed.*

*Another Christmas baby,*
*two thousand years before.*
*Saviour,*
*God-made-babe,*
*reaching through time to hold*
*hurting hearts and hands,*
*cradling my babe*
*in his scarred palms,*
*encircling my pain*
*in his outstretched arms,*
*replacing the death of hopes for the future,*
*with a different future.*

*My Christmas baby*
*has meaning*
*through the other Christmas baby.*
*My Christmas baby*
*lives*
*through the other Christmas baby,*
*and all he would become,*
*all he did,*
*on a cross,*
*far removed from the joy of his birth.*

*Remembering my Christmas baby,*
*but differently now,*
*knowing that the other Christmas baby,*
*who became*
*the perfect, Easter sacrifice,*
*feels my pain,*
*heals my pain,*
*loves me through the darkest valleys of remembrance*
*and draws me through,*
*stronger in his strength,*
*softer through his touch*
*in my heartbreak.*

*Christmas baby,*
*sinless saviour,*
*perfect sacrifice,*
*when the time comes*
*and forgetting gives way to remembering –*
*memories stir,*
*tears flow,*
*pain stabs –*
*remind me of the healing, joy, and hope,*
*shown so powerfully*
*to all men,*
*when you became*
*that Christmas baby,*
*who holds my Christmas baby*
*and all she left behind,*
*in your perfect, healing,*
*outstretched*
*hands.*

# 29 December

## Joseph loses his sense of safety

**After Herod died, an angel of the Lord appeared in a dream to Joseph in Egypt and said, 'Get up, take the child and his mother and go to the land of Israel, for those who were trying to take the child's life are dead.'**

**So he got up, took the child and his mother and went to the land of Israel. But when he heard that Archelaus was reigning in Judea in place of his father Herod, he was afraid to go there. Having been warned in a dream, he withdrew to the district of Galilee, and he went and lived in a town called Nazareth. So was fulfilled what was said through the prophets, that he would be called a Nazarene.**

MATTHEW 2:19–23

For the past 25 years or so, I have lived with myalgic encephalomyelitis, a disease that causes rapid muscle exhaustion after minimal exertion (among other issues). When I gave birth in 2010, the exertion of labour significantly worsened my condition. Now, I am mostly bed-bound.

In hospital after the birth, I was wracked with pain, constantly short of breath, and unable to stand without collapsing. Meanwhile, most of the nurses appeared cross that I took up a bed. Because the charts showed I hadn't lost too much blood, they assumed I was malingering. The combination of feeling unable to breathe along with medics denying and disbelieving my illness left me with PTSD. Though I'm finally receiving good counselling for it, I still experience dissociation and other symptoms when triggered. Each time, the same thought overwhelms my brain, 'I cannot go through this again.'

We may think of Bible heroes as somehow immune from mental illness, but Joseph is a wonderful example of a godly believer with probable PTSD.

Theologians estimate that the holy family lived in Egypt for around two years, with Herod dying in around 4BC. Joseph received the news of Herod's death via an angel in a dream, which seems to be God's preferred way of communicating important information to Joseph. The following is how I imagine Joseph felt. They make their long journey home, less urgently this time, but with those traumatic memories flooding back. As they get nearer, or perhaps as they enter the land and hear the latest from locals, Joseph learns that Herod has been replaced by his son, Archelaus. Perhaps this is when they hear about the massacre in Bethlehem.

Even though Joseph has received supernatural reassurance from an actual angel, his fear builds. When he approaches Bethlehem he thinks, 'I can't go through this again.' Like many people who have suffered trauma, he avoids the place where it happened.

I wonder how Joseph felt every year when they went to Jerusalem for Passover in the area Archelaus ruled (Luke 2:41). I wonder how Joseph felt that one time when Jesus was twelve, when they couldn't find him for three days.

Though I don't know of a patron saint for PTSD, I would love to nominate Joseph for this position. I find his story strangely soothing, realising that even Bible heroes don't necessarily feel okay after they've been rescued by God and the danger is over.

For this reason, I see God's compassion towards Joseph in what follows. Initially, God called Joseph home (v. 20). But Joseph 'was afraid to go there' (v. 22). God then gives him a second dream (v. 22), instructing him to go to Nazareth, where Jesus would grow up in relative obscurity. No doubt this was good protection for Jesus. I also suspect this was God's compassionate provision for Joseph, so he wouldn't wake up every day on hyper-alert, reliving his trauma again and again.

Sometimes the church can send the message that you should never fear anything because we have God. Joseph, however, gives us room for a bigger truth: that you can love God, have Jesus with you, and still have good reason to fear. To those who suffer from anxiety and PTSD, God gives compassion – and hopefully also a good therapist.

## Reflect

- What difference does it make to see Joseph as a survivor of trauma?
- To whom might you need to show compassion?

## Breath prayer

**Breathe in:** *I feel such dread and fear;*
**Breathe out:** *I will nestle beneath your wings.*

## 30 December

# Jesus will lose people's approval

**Now there was a man in Jerusalem called Simeon, who was righteous and devout. He was waiting for the consolation of Israel, and the Holy Spirit was on him. It had been revealed to him by the Holy Spirit that he would not die before he had seen the Lord's Messiah. Moved by the Spirit, he went into the temple courts. When the parents brought in the child Jesus to do for him what the custom of the Law required, Simeon took him in his arms and praised God, saying:**

**'Sovereign Lord, as you have promised,**
**you may now dismiss your servant in peace.**
**For my eyes have seen your salvation,**
**which you have prepared in the sight of all nations:**
**a light for revelation to the Gentiles,**
**and the glory of your people Israel.'**

**The child's father and mother marvelled at what was said about him. Then Simeon blessed them and said to Mary, his mother: 'This child is destined to cause the falling and rising of many in Israel, and to be a sign that will be spoken against, so that the thoughts of many hearts will be revealed.'**

LUKE 2:25–35A

Having left Mary and Joseph entering Nazareth perhaps five years after Jesus' birth, we now travel back in time, in Luke's gospel. In today's passage, Jesus has just been born, the shepherds' midnight visit was a few days ago, and Mary has recovered enough to venture into Jerusalem to make an offering for her firstborn, as the law said.

There is no threat yet from Herod, just the bewildering, wonderful state of new parenthood.

There in the temple, an older man waits for God's promise to be fulfilled: that he will see the Messiah before he dies. The statistics are surely against him, but God's Spirit is at work. The Spirit who promises is also the Spirit who engineers circumstances to keep those promises (vv. 26–27). Through this unlikely meeting, God blesses Simeon, who can now die rejoicing, and blesses Mary and Joseph, who collect another confirmation that their baby is the Messiah.

With the blessing, however, comes a warning, specifically to Mary. Some messianic prophecies foretold that God would rule peacefully from Jerusalem, and all peoples would flock to hear his wisdom (Isaiah 2:1–4; Micah 4:1–5). It sounds delightfully harmonious.

Simeon's warning is a reality check for Mary: Jesus would be highly divisive. Within God's people, Israel itself, Jesus would provoke the 'falling' (or downfall, ruin) of 'many', and the 'rising' (which can mean elevation or even resurrection) of others (v. 34).

On the one hand, Jesus would be 'a light' to the Gentiles, the glory of Israel and a 'sign' – a pledge, wonder or miracle (vv. 32, 34). On the other hand, he would be 'spoken against' or denied, opposed (v. 34).

We see this in Jesus' future ministry. He was beloved, yet betrayed; he was popular, then despised; religious leaders horribly maligned his motives and accused him of being a servant of Satan; he was mocked, threatened, and eventually killed.

On the surface, Jesus looked like a failure. Yet all people will be judged by their response to him: 'the thoughts of many hearts will be revealed' (v. 35). His followers, including common fishermen, prostitutes, disabled beggars, and children, were raised up within the kingdom of God, and the respected religious rulers were brought down.

If you have ever been unfairly spoken against, know that Jesus was, too. If you have ever been misunderstood, mocked, bullied, threatened, or abused by someone within the church, know the gift of God-with-us, who experienced that too. Though injustice often goes unchecked today, when Jesus returns there will be reckoning, and all hearts will be revealed.

## Reflect

- How do you feel when people turn against you unfairly?
- What difference does it make to recognise Jesus' divisiveness? How might this apply to the church today?

## Breath prayers

**Breathe in:** *Lord, when they lie and mock,*
**Breathe out:** *Reveal the truth of their hearts.*

**Breathe in:** *Lord, my light for revelation,*
**Breathe out:** *Jesus, please be my salvation.*

# 31 December

## Mary is given a glimpse of her future

**'And a sword will pierce your own soul too.'**

**There was also a prophet, Anna, the daughter of Penuel, of the tribe of Asher. She was very old; she had lived with her husband seven years after her marriage, and then was a widow until she was eighty-four. She never left the temple but worshipped night and day, fasting and praying. Coming up to them at that very moment, she gave thanks to God and spoke about the child to all who were looking forward to the redemption of Jerusalem.**

LUKE 2:35B–38

In my life, I find myself still reaching for the fairytale.

I am happily married, privileged to be a mother, and I find purpose and meaning in my writing. My life is so very nearly perfect.

I am also, more or less, bed-bound with chronic illness. Additionally, in 2021, my biggest fear was realised: my son was diagnosed with the same illness, triggered by Covid. It seems like at least one tragedy too many, especially when I know that God can heal miraculously.

In my faith, too, I reach for the fairytale.

I am thankful for the Bible's realism, and that when God lived on earth it was decidedly less smooth and harmonious than anything Disney would release.

Mary is as good a model as any for the reality of Christian living. She was shown great honour by God, highly favoured, and chosen to parent the second person of the Trinity, God incarnate. Prophets had sung songs over the baby in her womb, welcoming the Messiah who would bring peace, light, and salvation. After centuries of suffering, soon God would bring relief, and she would be part of it.

Only Simeon can whisper to her another part of the picture. Not only would Jesus be divisive, but Simeon's enigmatic prophecy about swords and souls hints that sorrow will come to Mary. As we look through the gospels, the last mention of Joseph is when Jesus is twelve. By the time Jesus begins his ministry, Mary is at the wedding in Cana, and she waits with Jesus' brothers when the crowds waylay Jesus, but Joseph is absent (John 2:1–11; Matthew 12:46–50). The most likely explanation is that Joseph has died.

Is it then a coincidence, that as soon as Simeon delivers his prophecy directly to Mary, the first person God puts across her path is someone known for being a widow? Anna was 84 and had only seven years of married life before becoming a widow. Yet this did not define her: she was a prophet who recognised the significance of Jesus. Not solely a prophet, she was primarily a worshipper who delighted in God and spent her days in the temple. Just as God gave Mary Elizabeth to encourage her when newly pregnant, so God gave Mary Anna as a model of how positive life could look as a widow.

There would be another sword-piercing of her soul, of course, when she stood at the cross, watching her son die an agonising death. Yet along with that agony, Jesus himself made provision for someone to support her after he ascended into heaven: the disciple John (John 19:25–27).

When I yearn for the fairytale in this present life, I remember Mary. I remember Jesus.

I also think of Frederick Buechner, novelist and theologian, who expresses those same gospel truths in our time:

> The grace of God means something like: 'Here is your life... Here is the world. Beautiful and terrible things will happen. Don't be afraid. I am with you. Nothing can ever separate us. It's for you I created the universe. I love you.'[24]

Though a sword may pierce our hearts, God never leaves us alone.

## Reflect

- Why do you think God gave Mary Simeon's prophecy about her own heartbreak?
- To what extent does Anna inspire you?

## Review

- Herod refused the gift of collaboration in favour of selfish power; Joseph lost his home and sense of safety but knew God's provision; the Bethlehemites mourned their children; Jesus' and Mary's futures contained grief and greatness. Whose stories have resonated with you the most? What has surprised you the most?
- How will these devotions influence how you deal with suffering? How will they influence the way you comfort others?

## Breath prayers

**Breathe in:** *Beautiful and terrible things happen;*
**Breathe out:** *Be with me always, O Lord.*

**Breathe in:** *A sword has pierced my heart;*
**Breathe out:** *Place your balm on my wounds, O Lord.*

6

# Living as losers

# Introduction

In 1999, Simon Guillebaud prayed: 'God, I surrender. I'll do anything and go anywhere.' Someone then told Simon he felt God was calling him to Burundi, Africa, which at the time was one of the most dangerous countries in the world. Sitting at the desk in his business job, Simon again prayed: 'If you want me to go to Burundi, give me a radical sign'. Immediately, the phone rang and the voice on the other end asked, 'Do you know anyone who wants to work in Burundi?'

Simon made the leap, moved continents, and started fundraising to create an organisation that facilitates locally led Burundian missions, bringing practical relief and spiritual transformation to the community. During the long civil war in Burundi, there were civilian massacres. With regular ambushes taking place along rebel-controlled roads he regularly used, life was so perilous that his proposal to his future wife included the question: 'Are you prepared to become a young widow?'

Thankfully, he was protected from the violence. Even so, he experienced loss from changing country and culture.

'On a shallow level, I really missed weddings,' he said of his early years there. Attending the weddings of dear family and friends meant flying back to Britain. Though he wouldn't make it a blanket rule for all missionaries, Simon couldn't stomach spending £800 on a flight when that money would literally save the lives of starving children around him, especially when his fledgling organisation was trying to raise vital funds.

Simon dismissed the loss of home comforts and diminished living standards as minor inconveniences but did acknowledge that poorer healthcare was a real sacrifice. He developed allergies and fighting for each breath every night was wearying. Eventually, when he had come to the end of his tether, he was treated successfully with a basic combination of western-acquired steroids, sobered by how quickly and easily it ended his suffering. Additionally, some friends he'd confided in and prayed with when Simon was new to the country turned out to be only interested in his access to money, and he was crushed when those relationships ended.

Manny Mvula was similarly called by God to leave his continent and culture, but in the reverse direction: from Zambia to Britain. He, too, has had to adapt, and has losses to contend with.

'I miss the unconditional love of and acceptance of people – regardless of your status,' Manny said. 'People in Africa have this great capacity to get you absorbed into their family or households. They always honour and bless visitors and travellers. I miss that type of love. Here, it's one man for himself. In Africa, we look after one another, even the stranger and foreigner.'

Despite these losses, however, both men rejoice in their calling. For Manny, coming to Britain meant coming to Christ, meeting his wife, and serving God as a couple through conservation projects, running an anti-trafficking charity, and evangelising in prisons and their local community. The gains of knowing God and using his gifts for God's kingdom were worth all the losses.

As for Simon, he rattles off the numerous blessings he's experienced in his less-travelled path: the joy of saving a woman from prostitution with just a $7 business loan; seeing street kids get education and hope; waking up each day with a real sense of purpose; the privilege of travel and seeing the world; the riches of deep friendships with extraordinary people from all countries and walks of life; and the realisation that stuff doesn't matter, people do. For Simon, it is not sacrifice, but privilege.

As we have seen, the nativity is not only about gifts and goodness. The individuals in the Christmas story suffered significant loss or disadvantage: Elizabeth and Zechariah with their years of infertility and Zechariah's silence; Mary's poverty, potential loss of reputation and her future bereavements; Joseph's hardship and trauma; the Magi leaving their home and the shepherds their sheep; Jesus losing the comforts of heaven; and the Bethlehem parents losing their children.

Christians are not immune to loss, and sometimes we're even called to further sacrifice. To live as a Christian means living as a loser. Jesus declared blessings over his followers – the meek, the mourning, the persecuted, and the dissatisfied. Early Christians were despised by intellectuals as weak-minded, expelled by religious authorities for being unorthodox, and locked up by the state for causing trouble.

If the Christian life is marked by as much loss as the next person, is it even worth it? This is a question Paul addresses in the letter to the Philippians. Like an accountant, he tots up the pluses and minuses, the losses and gains. The answer from Paul, as well as Simon and Manny, is a resounding, enthusiastic, exuberant yes. God pours out blessings on us.

As we enter a new year, with all the accompanying pressure to achieve, I invite you to a quick reset of perspective. We lift our eyes from the losses and gains of this life and re-evaluate them in the light of eternity. Even the worst of all losses, death, does not have the final word.

Above all, we see Jesus, the greatest gift, and how his love makes all the difference. This is a call to perseverance: it really is worth it. Come with me for this last lap of the race, and let's start the year with a renewed mind and refreshed spirit.

# 1 January

## Forget not his benefits

**Praise the Lord, my soul;**
**all my inmost being, praise his holy name.**
**Praise the Lord, my soul,**
**and forget not all his benefits –**
**who forgives all your sins**
**and heals all your diseases,**
**who redeems your life from the pit**
**and crowns you with love and compassion,**
**who satisfies your desires with good things**
**so that your youth is renewed like the eagle's.**
**The Lord works righteousness**
**and justice for all the oppressed.**
**He made known his ways to Moses,**
**his deeds to the people of Israel:**
**the Lord is compassionate and gracious,**
**slow to anger, abounding in love.**

PSALM 103:1–8

New Year can be a time of profound dissatisfaction. The high of Christmas and the partying of New Year's Eve is over, and the year looms before us. We look at what's lacking in our lives and make resolutions to fix it all. This new year will be bigger and better than the last, we tell ourselves.

The antidote to dissatisfaction is gratitude. When we first applied for house and contents insurance, we had to audit all that we owned.

Room by room, I went through the house looking at all my possessions, one by one, recording their value. It took me longer than I intended, because I kept getting distracted by things I'd forgotten. The Richard Scarry storybook I'd loved as a child; the earrings Jon had bought me for Christmas and hidden in a Christmas cracker to surprise me; the poem a dear friend had written for me that always made me cry; the placemats we'd carefully chosen just after we got married – all these little things held precious memories. By the end of the exercise, I was overwhelmed. Just look at what I already have, I thought.

Paying attention to our blessings increases our awareness of goodness, naming those blessings increases our gratitude, and gratitude increases our joy. This is precisely what David does in this psalm. He gives himself two instructions: to praise the Lord (v. 1) and to 'forget not all his benefits' (v. 2). He then starts listing as many blessings as he can. Interestingly, he doesn't name tangible, material things that I might first be thankful for (a good job, a comfortable house, or nice family and friends). Instead, he lists spiritual blessings.

David praises God for life-saving redemption, forgiveness of sins, good, satisfying things, and ongoing renewal of youthful energy (vv. 3–5). My mind trips over the part about healing all diseases, since I am not healed from chronic illness and know so many others with debilitating conditions. At the same time, however, I recognise that God does occasionally heal miraculously, and disease will not have the last word even if not healed in this life, for there will be no pain in heaven (Revelation 21:4).

Recognising that all is not well in the world, David also thanks God for working to bring 'justice for all the oppressed' (v. 6), and for making God's purpose and plans known, so we are not in the dark (v. 7). David describes, with beautiful poetry, how our gracious God, 'abounding in love', crowns us 'with love and compassion' (vv. 8, 4).

As we have walked through the Christmas story, we have been unwrapping some of these hidden, spiritual gifts: honour, when the world views you with shame; favour, when the world has forgotten you; songs of joy after being silenced; support from God through the arms of others; guidance when you are under threat; provision when you are needy; comfort for when you mourn. Additionally, as people living on the other side of Christ's resurrection, we have the assurance of the Holy Spirit – God with us, helping us, all the time.

'Forget not his benefits', David urges us. I invite you to pause and praise God for all these gifts and more. Just look at what we already have.

## Reflect

- What's on your 'spiritual blessing inventory'? It may help to write the blessings down.
- For which of these are you especially thankful today?
- Meditate on Ephesians 1:3.

## Pray

*I praise you and rejoice, my God,*
*for blessing me in the heavenly realms*
*where no one can snatch that treasure away.*
*I praise you and rejoice, King Jesus,*
*for every spiritual blessing I find in you:*
*your abundant love, your well of compassion,*
*the crown you place on my head.*
*May I remember to thank you*
*and not forget all your benefits –*
*just look at all I already have.*
*Amen.*

## 2 January

# What Jesus lost and gained

**Do nothing out of selfish ambition or vain conceit. Rather, in humility value others above yourselves, not looking to your own interests but each of you to the interests of the others.**

**In your relationships with one another, have the same mindset as Christ Jesus:**

**who, being in very nature God,**
**did not consider equality with God something to be used to his own advantage;**
**rather, he made himself nothing**
**by taking the very nature of a servant,**
**being made in human likeness.**
**And being found in appearance as a man,**
**he humbled himself**
**by becoming obedient to death –**
**even death on a cross!**
**Therefore God exalted him to the highest place**
**and gave him the name that is above every name…**

PHILIPPIANS 2:3–9

At this time of year, the world shouts at us – seize every opportunity! Let this be the year of me! Fight for that promotion! As I look through the news, I see a world that values and promotes those who are openly selfish in their ambition. Look after number one, we are told. When we see the wicked prosper by prioritising themselves, pushing others down on their way to the top, we begin to believe the only way to succeed is to play the world's game.

Paul speaks into this mindset. Warning people against 'selfish ambition' (v. 3), he points to Christ's example. If anyone deserved to be celebrated for who he was and use it to their advantage, it was Jesus. He was, after all, God. Yet Jesus' journey to earth was a downward leap, shedding privilege and protection along the way. The king became a 'servant'; the one who is everything became a 'nothing' (v. 7). This wasn't humility for its own sake but to save people through his death on the cross.

Therefore, God exalted him. God has a long-standing habit of exalting the humble and elevating the worthy. No one has ever been more deserving, and therefore no one humbler, than the creator of the world who became a creature. It follows, then, that Christ becomes the most exalted of all. This is how God balances the universe, at least at the end of time.

To be a Christian means quietly meeting others' needs and letting God do the glorifying, instead of seeking glory for ourselves. But what does this look like in practice? I cannot think of a more perfect example of humility in action than my husband, Jon. He has an uncanny knack of seeing and meeting others' needs before they've even had to ask. If he meets anyone who needs a bin moved, a meal cooked, or a problem solved, he just does it. He also cares for two disabled family members without complaining to us – though he's welcome to complain elsewhere!

Don't get me wrong: his ego is well and truly intact, and he has a great sideline in sardonic humour. He has plenty of ambition, but crucially no 'selfish ambition' (v. 3). We think humble must mean self-effacing with low self-esteem, but Jesus knew his own power and ability and was comfortable in it. Rather, Jesus shows us the value of being downwardly mobile, not to chase praise and prestige from humans but from God.

Philippians 2:4 can be translated as: 'Let each of you look out *not only* for his own interests, *but also* for the interests of others' (NKJV, italics added). So this doesn't mean we allow people to abuse us in the name of valuing others above ourselves. Instead, we leave space in our lives for meeting others' needs as well as pursuing our own interests, as Jesus did in his ministry. In a world that says, 'Look out for number one', we look out for others and listen for God's prompting.

## Reflect

- How do we balance looking out for our own needs and the needs of others?
- How does Jesus' downward-mission reshape your ambitions for this year?
- Meditate on 2 Corinthians 8:9.

## Pray

*Jesus, you gave up your heavenly throne,*
*becoming poor, that I might be rich.*
*O Lord, may my ambition not be selfish.*
*May I meet others' needs without grumbling,*
*and receive without feeling ashamed.*
*Amen.*

## 3 January

# What we cannot lose

**What, then, shall we say in response to these things? If God is for us, who can be against us?… Who will bring any charge against those whom God has chosen? It is God who justifies. Who then is the one who condemns? No one. Christ Jesus who died – more than that, who was raised to life – is at the right hand of God and is also interceding for us. Who shall separate us from the love of Christ? Shall trouble or hardship or persecution or famine or nakedness or danger or sword?…**

**No, in all these things we are more than conquerors through him who loved us. For I am convinced that neither death nor life, neither angels nor demons, neither the present nor the future, nor any powers, neither height nor depth, nor anything else in all creation, will be able to separate us from the love of God that is in Christ Jesus our Lord.**

ROMANS 8:31, 33–35, 37–39

Has anyone ever falsely accused you or called your motives into question? The sting of injustice is intense, and, without vindication, this can haunt us. It is a horrible feeling to be misunderstood.

Yew knows this all too well. As a Christian from Southeast Asia, he felt called to move to China with his wife, work there, and be a faithful witness to Christ. They started a business and a family and lived a happy, settled life in China for 20 years, expecting to stay there forever.

One day, out of the blue, the police came. Because he was a Christian worker, Yew and his wife were suspected and accused of being malicious agents for hostile western governments. They were subjected to days of intense questioning, followed by weeks of investigation. Finally, they were apparently found harmless enough but were forced out of the country nevertheless, with no opportunity to say goodbye.

'What caught me completely off-guard,' Yew reflected later, 'was the sense of shame.' When he and his wife were marched away by police, his trusted employees, for whom he cared deeply, looked back with hardened, angry faces. The neighbours glared at them with disdain.

Then, the police played dizzying psychological games during the hours of interrogation so that Yew began to question, then feel deeply ashamed, of his calling. Most of the questioning centred on other Christian workers whom China might want to similarly accuse of being spies, and Yew feared inadvertently giving away details that might endanger others and destroy their work. The shame if that occurred was almost too much to contemplate.

He thought of Shadrach, Meshach, and Abednego's trial in the fiery furnace (Daniel 3:16–28) and prayed he would emerge from the flames of questioning without endangering others or denying God. Mercifully, God answered his prayer. After some time, his feelings shifted. 'My hair was not singed nor my clothes tainted with the smell of shame,' he said.

The apostle Paul was falsely accused, too: of speaking against the Jewish law and people, desecrating the temple, and starting riots as a seditious 'troublemaker' (Acts 24:5–8). Paul, too, was misunderstood and maligned by the leaders of his own beloved country. His theology in this passage is borne from painful experience.

It's as if Paul lifts our eyes above all earthly rule, till its leaders are ant-small, and asks from the perspective of eternity and the heavenly realms – who is the judge here? To Christians, like Yew, bruised by the shame of false charges, Paul emphatically declares that any accusation, condemnation, or threat is absolutely meaningless and powerless in the face of God's approval. God is for us, so whatever comes against us is ridiculous in comparison, like a weasel trying to fight a tank. 'If God is for us, who can be against us?' (v. 31).

Yew lost almost everything: his home, friends, community, business, and the only 'hometown' his children had known. He lost what he imagined to be his future, and he has had to lament that loss. 'Our roots to the place and people ran deep and they were severed suddenly', Yew explained. 'I still nurse the cut and broken ends.'

Yet his hope, and ours, rests in God, who is above all earthly powers and comforts us in our sorrows. What Yew cannot lose, what can never be snatched away from any of us, is 'the love of God that is in Jesus Christ our Lord' (v. 39). Even the world's most devastating 'no' to us can never cancel out God's emphatic 'yes'.

## Reflect

- In which ways has the world said 'no' to you? How can you remind yourself of God's 'yes'?
- What does it mean to you that you can never lose God's love?

## Pray

*Dear God,*
*when I am misunderstood,*
*let me rest in the love of the one who knows me best.*
*When I am falsely accused,*
*let me rest in the love of the heavenly judge.*
*When I face hostile stares,*
*let me rest in the love of the one who sees me.*
*May I know your undefeated, indefatigable, unwavering love today.*
*Amen.*

# 4 January

## To die is gain?

**I eagerly expect and hope that I will in no way be ashamed, but will have sufficient courage so that now as always Christ will be exalted in my body, whether by life or by death. For to me, to live is Christ and to die is gain. If I am to go on living in the body, this will mean fruitful labour for me. Yet what shall I choose? I do not know! I am torn between the two: I desire to depart and be with Christ, which is better by far; but it is more necessary for you that I remain in the body.**

PHILIPPIANS 1:20–24

It is quite some claim to state that death is a 'gain'. Paul wrote to the Philippians from prison, probably in Rome, in around AD60. Considering his circumstances, this is a relentlessly optimistic letter, ending in an exhortation to rejoice (Philippians 4:4). In this passage, he's writing to reassure the Christians back in Philippi that he doesn't think he will be killed yet, but even if he is, they are not to worry on his account. 'For to me,' Paul explains, 'to live is Christ and to die is gain' (v. 21). In fact, he would even welcome death, because it would mean being with Christ, 'which is better by far' (v. 23). His sole reason for living is to continue his ministry.

When applying this to ourselves, we need to remember Paul's caveat: 'For to me' (v. 21). He is not setting forth a universal rule, and his situation was quite special: unmarried, with no mention of close friends or community needing him for support. After his conversion his singular purpose (and unique calling) was to preach about Jesus, and that shaped everything.

This phrase is not the only thing the Bible, or even Paul, says about death. Death is 'the last enemy to be destroyed' (1 Corinthians 15:26), and Jesus wept, rather than celebrated, at Lazarus' tomb (John 11:35). For everyone, death is loss. But if we are Christians, death is not solely loss, it is also gain.

When Steve Legg, a loving and sunny-natured evangelist, was given a terminal diagnosis of cancer, he was more positive about the news than many of his friends. Although he choked up with tears at the thought of leaving his wife, adult children, and grandchild, he himself held no fear of dying, and adopted Paul's words as his own. Facing death increased his faith and sharpened his love for Jesus.

'I'm in a win–win situation,' Steve explained. 'If I beat this, then I've won. And if I don't, I go to be with Jesus, and I've won. I can't fail!'[25]

After Steve died, his widow, Bekah, also found fresh comfort in Paul's words, 'To die is gain.' For the first time, she felt like she had one foot in heaven, while still loving life on earth. 'I've got stakes in both worlds now,' she said. 'Wherever I am, I'm missing somebody, and wherever I am, I've got someone I love.'

Bekah found that Steve's death opened her eyes to the reality of heaven. 'Heaven has become much more tangible to me now because I can imagine being back with Steve,' she explained. 'Long term, I know it will be more exciting to see Jesus in heaven than my husband. Yet my longing to be with Steve helps me feel, in a real way, how much better it will be with Jesus in heaven. I can't wait to see Jesus face to face.'

Death is still the great destroyer, but it does not have the final word. If today you feel overwhelmed by the shadow of death, remember that this life is but the overture: the great concerto is yet to begin.

## Reflect

- What verses comfort you when you think about death?

## Pray

Use this verse as a basis for meditative prayer:

> *Yea, though I walk through the valley of the shadow of death,*
> *I will fear no evil;*
> *For You are with me;*
> *Your rod and Your staff, they comfort me.*
> PSALM 23:4 (NKJV)

# 5 January

## Everything is loss

**If someone else thinks they have reasons to put confidence in the flesh, I have more: circumcised on the eighth day, of the people of Israel, of the tribe of Benjamin, a Hebrew of Hebrews; in regard to the law, a Pharisee; as for zeal, persecuting the church; as for righteousness based on the law, faultless.**

**But whatever were gains to me I now consider loss for the sake of Christ. What is more, I consider everything a loss because of the surpassing worth of knowing Christ Jesus my Lord, for whose sake I have lost all things. I consider them garbage, that I may gain Christ and be found in him, not having a righteousness of my own that comes from the law, but that which is through faith in Christ – the righteousness that comes from God on the basis of faith.**

PHILIPPIANS 3:4B–9

During the Christmas holidays when I was 17, most people my age were frantically revising for their A-level mock exams – or out partying. I was lying in my bed, trying to rest but also worrying. I hadn't recovered well from mononucleosis, but I kept studying, despite my exhaustion. Looking back, pushing myself likely caused permanent damage to my body. But even if you warned 17-year-old me of these potential consequences, I doubt I would have acted differently.

Partly, this was because of the relentless messaging educators give to children at school: *This is your future! Everything depends on these grades! Work harder! The world is competitive! Do your best! Your very best! And some extracurricular activities, too! These are the happiest days of your life, by the way!*

Partly, I had a drive to excel. Academic work always came naturally to me, so it became a precious part of my identity. By the time I reached my A levels, that ambition had twisted into a compulsion to get four A grades and go to the University of Cambridge or it all meant nothing. Meanwhile, I was also trying to excel as a Christian, getting up early to read the Bible and pray, witnessing to my friends, and staying away from temptations. My genuine love for Jesus was mixed up with my desire to prove myself. It never felt quite enough.

If you have ever felt that impetus to prove yourself to others, whether it's about having the right qualifications, moving in the right circles, getting the right job, showing your toughness, being the perfect parent, succeeding in the eyes of the world, or being respected within the church, this is the passage for you.

Paul knew that feeling like no one else. He ticked all the boxes for success: the right family, the right heritage, respected as an educated Pharisee, an expert in the law (vv. 4b–5). He was also born a Roman citizen, so he carried that societal privilege too. But note his obsession with moral perfection: he was so desperate to appear righteous that he scrupulously kept the Jewish law and turned to violent extremism in the name of religion (v. 6).

In his accounting journal, however, Paul now realises that he spent a long time pursuing worthless achievements. He ratchets it up for emphasis: these supposed gains are 'loss' (v. 7), in fact everything is 'loss' (v. 8), and finally he declares it is all 'garbage' (v. 8), a word in Greek so crude that some translators think our curse-word meaning faeces might be a better translation.

He never needed qualifications, status, prestige; he needed Christ. Instead of a *performative* righteousness, 'a righteousness of my own' (v. 9), he now has a *gifted* righteousness from Christ. He has exchanged the exhaustion of trying to impress everyone with the assurance of righteousness and approval from Jesus, which he does not have to earn.

I still feel the pull to prove myself from time to time, but I am learning to rest in Christ. All these ambitions – they can be unhealthy or healthy distractions, but they are never the main event. We are already declared righteous. We have all the qualifications we need.

## Reflect

- To whom do you feel the need to prove yourself?
- As you consider what drives you, how much of that derives from insecurity?
- What does 'the surpassing worth of knowing Christ' (v. 8) mean to you?
- Meditate on Jesus' words in Matthew 11:28.

## Pray

*When the weariness of trying so hard*
*to be good*
*weighs upon me,*
*let me rest on the pillow of your righteousness.*
*When I am burdened*
*by my failures and frustrations,*
*let me rest on the shoulder of my Saviour.*
*Be with me Jesus.*
*I release the dross of empty achievement,*
*and I treasure, like gold, the worth of knowing you.*
*Amen.*

## 6 January

# The greatest gain

**I want to know Christ – yes, to know the power of his resurrection and participation in his sufferings, becoming like him in his death, and so, somehow, attaining to the resurrection from the dead.**

**Not that I have already obtained all this, or have already arrived at my goal, but I press on to take hold of that for which Christ Jesus took hold of me. Brothers and sisters, I do not consider myself yet to have taken hold of it. But one thing I do: forgetting what is behind and straining towards what is ahead, I press on towards the goal to win the prize for which God has called me heavenwards in Christ Jesus.**

PHILIPPIANS 3:10–14

My father, Martin, became a Christian in his 20s and hasn't looked back since. In his early days of faith, the phrase 'Seek first the kingdom of God', became a motto for him (Matthew 6:33a, NKJV). Initially, he and my mum prayerfully considered becoming missionaries, but the doors didn't open for them. He was a lawyer by profession, and he realised his calling was to be a solicitor who reflected Christ.

When he was a criminal lawyer, if his client confessed to the crime, he would generally advise them to be honest about it.

'My job as a lawyer was to act in my client's best interests. My convictions as a Christian are to value truth,' he explained. 'Yet there was rarely a conflict between the two. Pleading guilty was generally in my client's long-term best interests, as the evidence was against them, and they got a far more lenient sentence than if they had denied their crime.'

His clients were grateful for his honesty about their best chances, and one time, a criminal was so struck by Martin's faith that he (and subsequently his whole family) became Christians too. When Martin switched to property law, he charged a fair price for his time, but where the job had taken more hours than expected and the client was poor, he billed them less. When dealing with opponents, he was firm and persistent but never abusive or mean. After retirement, he supported an international justice charity.

An infectiously positive person and an instinctive evangelist, he also looked for every opportunity to talk about Jesus. Today, he serves alongside my mum in multiple ways at church, including a preaching ministry. My dad has always wanted Jesus to shape every aspect of his life. He embodies Paul's phrase, 'to live is Christ' (Philippians 1:21).

Paul wrote today's passage from prison, his life under threat. He realised he could die soon but was making the most of the present (Philippians 1:19–26). In fact, historians estimate he died two-to-five years after writing Philippians. Having reviewed his past and counted it as loss, Paul didn't become disheartened. Instead, he fixed his eyes forward, 'forgetting what is behind and straining towards what is ahead' (v. 13). For anyone who feels they wasted time in their former years, this is an encouragement to think positively about the future.

Of course, the future, for the Christian, includes eternity, not just our time on earth. Like Paul, our goal is heaven, our prize is resurrection and our future is everlasting life (vv. 10, 14).

How do we live with that focus in mind? Like Paul, my dad may be nearing the end of his life. Diagnosed with a rare cancer a few years ago, his prognosis is unknown, and he is already defying most survival statistics with a smile on his face.

'When I was younger, I was quite excited about dying and going to heaven,' he told me. 'When the reality of this diagnosis sank in, I was less keen about the prospect in practice than I was in theory!'

He gave a wry grin.

'But now – now, I can just about picture it,' he said carefully. 'I'm prepared. Till then, I want to go on serving. I already know the Christian life is a marathon, not a sprint, and I want to continue that race to the end.'

What Martin brings is a clarity to living as a Christian: to know Jesus, love Jesus, serve Jesus in whichever way best fits our personality and circumstances, and to look forward to meeting Jesus.

As we start this new year, the best resolution to make is probably Paul's: 'I want to know Christ' (v. 10). There is no experience in life that is not better faced with Jesus beside us.

I also want to know 'the power of his resurrection' (v.10), through little glimpses during this life and the triumphant reversal of destruction at the end. I want to remember that whatever else life throws at us, it is Jesus upon whom history hinges, Jesus who brings gifts of joy and blessing, and Jesus who will carry us through death's darkness into his wondrous light. As you look to the coming year, I offer this to you: Jesus – just Jesus – our best gift and our greatest gain.

## Reflect

- Imagine Paul's 'accounting journal' of losses and gains. On one side, write the losses and gains you're facing now. On the other, write the spiritual gifts we have in Christ. How does it feel to do this?
- To what extent does Jesus feel like the greatest gift in your life? Why do you think this is?
- Living for Christ means knowing Jesus, loving Jesus, serving Jesus, and looking forward to meeting to Jesus. Which of these four do you feel most called to focus on this year?
- If Christ were in front of you right now, what would you say?

## Review

- As you think back through this whole book, what have you learned?
- As you think back through the book, how have you changed?
- Which section has been your favourite? Why?
- What will you take away with you from this book?

## Pray

*Dear Lord Jesus,*
*thank you for all your gifts to me.*
*Thank you for your kindness and presence*
*when life's hardships bruise or wound me.*
*Thank you for being with me, Immanuel.*
*Amen.*

# Acknowledgements

The making of this book has depended on many amazing people willing to give their time and heart to share their stories with me, and I am profoundly grateful to every one of you. Your stories have changed me, and I thank you. Most of the people with surnames included are writers, and you should definitely check out their books.

Thank you to BRF Ministries for being a wonderful publisher, especially Olivia Warburton, who twisted my arm, Rachel Tranter for your flexibility and support, Daniele Och for being the kindest project manager I could hope for, and Rose Edwards for listening so well in her art. This book, as is the case for all my work, is organic writing, without the use of generative AI.

Thank you to Jenny Rowbory, author of *The Winter People*, my dear friend by whom I measure the effectiveness of all my theology. Thank you to my spirit-sisters, the Elizabeths to my Mary and vice versa, without whom I could not write: Amy Robinson and Amy Boucher Pye, Beth Fite and Abby Norman, all of whom are brilliant writers themselves. Special thanks to my husband and son, who suffer for my art, and who bore with me in my 'book tunnel' and three months of FFP3 masks.

Thank you for reading: please do leave a review wherever you purchased it, which is gold dust for authors.

# Select Bibliography

Zeba Crook, 'Honor, shame, and social status revisited', *Journal of Biblical Literature* 128.3 (2009), pp. 591–611, **doi.org/10.2307/25610205**

Zeba Crook, *The Ancient Mediterranean Social World: A source book* (William B. Eerdmans, 2020).

Linda Fletcher, 'Discovering the place of shame in the gospel through witness and co-creation of female trauma survivors', *Anvil Journal of Theology and Mission* 37.2 (2021), **churchmissionsociety.org/anvil/discovering-the-place-of-shame-in-the-gospel-through-witness-and-co-creation-with-female-trauma-survivors-linda-fletcher-anvil-vol-37-issue-2**

Paula Gooder, *The Meaning Is in the Waiting: The Spirit of Advent* (Canterbury Press, 2008).

Paula Gooder, *Journey to the Manger: Exploring the birth of Jesus* (Fortress Press, 2016).

Joel B. Green, 'The social status of Mary in Luke 1,5-2,52: a plea for methodological integration', *Biblica* 73.4 (1992), pp. 457–72.

Paul L. Maier, 'Herod and the infants of Bethlehem', *Chronos, Kairos, Christos II: Chronological, nativity, and religious studies in memory of Ray Summers*, edited by E. Jerry Vardaman (Mercer University Press, 1998), pp. 169–89.

Bruce J. Malina, *The New Testament World: Insights from cultural anthropology* (Westminster John Knox Press, 2001).

Claude Mariotinni, 'Israel in Exile', Dr Claude Mariottini – Professor of Old Testament Blog, 18 July 2016. **claudemariottini.com/2016/07/18/israel-in-exile**

John J. Pilch and Bruce Malina (ed.), *Handbook of Biblical Social Values*, third edition (Wipf and Stock, 2016).

Frank Reilly, 'Jane Schaberg, Raymond E. Brown, and the Problem of the Illegitimacy of Jesus.' *Journal of Feminist Studies in Religion* 21.1 (2005), pp. 57–80, **jstor.org/stable/25002516**

Judith Rossall, 'Whose honour? Whose shame?', *Anvil Journal of Theology and Mission* 37.2 (2021), **churchmissionsociety.org/anvil/whose-honour-whose-shame-some-reflections-on-the-bible-judith-rossall-anvil-vol-37-issue-2**

Carolyn J. Sharp, 'The holy innocents: commentary on Jeremiah 31:15–17', The Working Preacher website, 28 December 2014, **workingpreacher.org/commentaries/revised-common-lectionary/the-holy-innocents/commentary-on-jeremiah-3115-17**

Carlton Turner, 'Legacies and chains: structuring shame in the African Caribbean', *Anvil Journal of Theology and Mission* 37.2 (2021), **churchmissionsociety.org/anvil/legacies-and-chains-structuring-shame-in-the-african-caribbean-carlton-turner-anvil-vol-37-issue-2/**

# Guidance and discussion questions for group study

Although this book is written for personal devotions that start on 1 December, bitter experience has taught me that no one turns up for a small group after the beginning of December. There is just too much else going on.

My advice for small group leaders, therefore, is to start this series in **early-to-mid November**, so there is ample time for four weekly sessions before the madness of Christmastide hits. If you meet fortnightly, adjust accordingly. Small group members should also ignore the dates on the devotions and take each segment week by week. This way, you reach the end of reading part 4, 'Giving up' (perhaps aptly named), in early-to-mid December. Parts 5 and 6, 'Pierced hearts' and 'Living as losers', can then be read over Christmas or the first week of January, with one session to cover both these sections, **ending the series in the second week of January**.

Both the 'checking in' and the discussion questions are shaped by the overall themes of the book: 'grief and gift' running together, or 'loss and gain' where that's more appropriate. In addition to the discussion questions, the session will end with a form of *lectio divina*, using one of the passages from the devotions, which you can omit if short of time. Allow approximately 15–25 minutes for this, depending on your tolerance for silence and repetition.

For each session, bring *Treasures in Straw*, a Bible, pen and paper for reflective doodling, if desired, and appropriate music, if required. Leaders, there are more questions than will likely fill an hour, so feel free to be selective.

# Session 1: Kingdom reversals

## Preparation

Read the Introduction and part 1, 'Kingdom reversals'.

## 1 Checking in: grief and gift

- Share with each other something good that's happened this week or something hard, or both.

## 2 Introduction: grief and gift

- How do you usually find Christmastime? What do you struggle with? What do you love about it? (All answers are welcomed.)

- To what extent can you relate to having to hide your grief for the sake of others? What do you feel about the author's call to honesty at Christmastime?

## 3 Kingdom reversals: grief and gift

- Christmas is about Jesus' coming to people who live in darkness; the hopeless, the forgotten, the battle-weary, the overlooked. To what extent are you currently struggling with these issues? (Only share as much as you feel comfortable with.)

- Christmas is about 'kingdom reversals' – the little become great and vice versa, the dark see light, the burdened are released, those caught up in war receive peace. To what extent have you seen these reversals in your own experience? Thinking about the world, which countries or peoples do you long to receive these reversals? Although Christ came to bring peace to all people, we don't yet see that. How do you make sense of the 'now' and the 'not yet' of God's kingdom? Thinking about your community, which reversals do you long to see?

- Thinking of God's gifts of: light; peace; release from burden; being noticed by God; a hopeful future – which of these do you need at the moment? Which are you most thankful for (if this is different)?

## 4 Lectio divina

1 **Read**: one person reads Isaiah 9:1–7 while the rest listen.

2 **Meditate**: hear the passage again, listening for a key word or phrase that specifically speaks to you. Pause prayerfully at the end of the passage, keeping silence or doodling.

3 **Share** (optional): share with one another your key word or phrase and why it has resonated with you.

4 **Prayer** (out loud or in silence): pray, praise, or lament, reflecting on the passage.

5 **Contemplation**: have a moment of silence or listen to 'His yoke is easy' from Handel's *Messiah* or 'He who is mighty' by Rebecca Elliott and Kate DeGraide.

6 **Close**: choose a written prayer (e.g. 1 December) and say it together.

# Session 2: Honour and favour

## Preparation

Read the whole of part 2, 'Honour and favour'.

## 1 Checking in: grief and gift

- Share with each other something good that's happened this week or something hard, or both.

## 2 Honour and favour: grief and gift

- How familiar are you with honour/shame cultures around the world? What can we learn from them? To what extent is honour/shame present in our society? What difference has it made to read these passages through this lens?

- 'Shame is the cloud that society arbitrarily blows on to us.' What struck you about Inger's story? What do you think the difference is between being 'shamed' and being 'ashamed'? How do you deal with either? Where in your life have you encountered either being honoured or being shamed, either justly or unjustly? What helps you have a right perspective in this? What difference does it make to know that Jesus experienced shame and dishonour?

- What are the ways we honour others today? Who in your community or the world at large could you honour? What do you think the difference is between honour and favour? To what extent is it a comfort to know that God honours us if society rejects us?

- Consider Elizabeth, Mary, and Zechariah in these passages: to whom do you most relate? Whose story has taught you the most this week, and why? How might that change you?

## 3 Lectio divina

1 **Read**: one person reads Luke 1:26–30 while the rest listen.

2 **Meditate**: hear the passage again, listening for a key word or phrase that specifically speaks to you. Pause prayerfully at the end of the passage, keeping silence or doodling.

3 **Share** (optional): share with one another your key word or phrase and why it has resonated with you.

4 **Prayer** (out loud or in silence): pray, praise, or lament, reflecting on the passage.

5 **Contemplation**: have a moment of silence or listen to 'The Lord bless you and keep you' by John Rutter or 'The Blessing' by Cody Carnes, Elevation Worship, and Kari Jobe.

6 **Close**: choose a written prayer (e.g. 5, 8, or 9 December) and say it together.

# Session 3: Songs after silence

## Preparation

Read the whole of part 3, 'Songs after silence'.

## 1 Checking in: grief and gift

- Share with each other something good that's happened this week or something hard, or both.

## 2 Songs after silence: grief and gift

- What struck you about Bekah's story? Read aloud the section on silences from the introduction. How do you feel in general about silence? What kind of 'bad' silences have you experienced? When has silence been a gift to you?

- Which communities or individuals close to your heart do you feel have been silenced? (Beware of getting side-tracked on politics!) What practical steps might we take to highlight their needs?

- God's prophets were silent for 400 years before the flurry of activity in Jesus' arrival. To what extent do you find this encouraging or discouraging? When have you experienced God's silence when you have prayed, and what was this like for you? What things does God seem to be silent on at the moment? What helps you when God is silent?

- Luke's gospel is full of songs and prayers. How did the practice of (literal) singing this week affect you? What difference does it make to see either good silences or songs as gifts from God? As you look back at the different types of songs, which have you most needed to hear? And which songs has God given you to sing in this season?

## 3 Lectio divina

1 **Read**: one person reads Luke 1:76–79 while the rest listen.

2 **Meditate**: hear the passage again, listening for a key word or phrase that specifically speaks to you. Pause prayerfully at the end of the passage, keeping silence or doodling.

3 **Share** (optional): share with one another your key word or phrase and why it has resonated with you.

4 **Prayer** (out loud or in silence): pray, praise or lament, reflecting on the passage.

5 **Contemplation**: have a moment of silence, sing your favourite version of 'Come thou long expected Jesus' by Charles Wesley or 'Light of the world' by Lauren Daigle, or listen to classical arrangements of the Magnificat or 'The people that walked in darkness' from Handel's *Messiah*. Perhaps dim the lights and light a candle or two during this time.

6 **Close**: choose a written prayer (e.g. 17 or 18 December) and say it together.

# Session 4: Giving up

## Preparation

Read the Introduction and part 4, 'Giving up'.

## 1 Checking in: loss and gain

- Share with each other something good that's happened this week or something hard, or both.

## 2 Giving up: loss and gain

- What struck you about Cara's story? How might you adapt your Christmas practices to find joy this year? In this season, what have you been called to give up (quit), give up (sacrifice), or give upwards (surrender)? How has that been? When in your life have you sacrificed something or lost something only to receive something greater in return? Or when have you learnt to appreciate smaller gifts after a great loss?

- Jesus gave up heaven to become Immanuel. What does the incarnation mean to you? In what areas of your life are you thankful to have 'God with us'? What difference does it make to see Jesus himself, rather than his benefits, as the greatest gift?

- Joseph gave up his rights yet gained a family and a far greater honour. Mary had her comfort and dignity taken from her but was honoured by foreign dignitaries. The shepherds risked their sheep to find their Shepherd. The Magi left their home and gave up precious things but were guided by God and found great joy. Which of those characters has most challenged or encouraged you? What gifts – material, relational, and spiritual – are you thankful for in this season?

## 3 Lectio divina

1 **Read**: one person reads Luke 2:15–20 while the rest listen.

2 **Meditate**: hear the passage again, listening for a key word or phrase that specifically speaks to you. Pause prayerfully at the end of the passage, keeping silence or doodling.

3 **Share** (optional): share with one another your key word or phrase and why it has resonated with you.

4 **Prayer** (out loud or in silence): pray, praise, or lament, reflecting on the passage.

5 **Contemplation**: have a moment of silence or listen to/sing 'The angels and the shepherds' (arr. C.H. Trevor, sung by the Choir of Kings College Cambridge), 'Hark the herald angels sing' by Charles Wesley, or 'Emmanuel God with us' by Chris Tomlin.

6 **Close**: choose a written prayer (e.g. 25 December) and say it together.

# Session 5: Pierced hearts and living as losers

## Preparation

Read part 5, 'Pierced hearts', and part 6, 'Living as losers'.

## 1 Checking in: loss and gain

- Share with each other something good that's happened this week or something hard, or both.

## 2 Pierced hearts: grief and gift

- What most impacted you from reading this section? How did your view of the Bible characters change?

- What were your reflections on Abby's story? If you are comfortable, consider sharing your own story of grief and what helped.

- Grief counsellor Lois Tonkin created the 'growing around grief model'. Rather than grief shrinking as time goes on, many people find their grief stays the same 'size' but gradually other gifts in life are added around it, making life more pleasurable. How do you see this in the lives of Joseph and Mary, or your own?

## 3 Living as losers: loss and gain

- What inspires you about Simon and Manny's stories? What practices do you have to 'count your blessings'? What difference does this practice make to you? What three things are you thankful for today and what three spiritual blessings mean a lot to you?

- How does having a spiritual perspective affect your resolutions for this year? What's your relationship like with ambition?

- As you think through this book, which section has meant the most to you? How have these readings changed your thinking or practices? What message will you take away with you from these devotions?

## 4 Lectio divina

1. **Read**: one person reads Psalm 103:1–8 while the rest listen.

2. **Meditate**: hear the passage again, listening for a key word or phrase that specifically speaks to you. Pause prayerfully at the end of the passage, keeping silence or doodling.

3. **Share** (optional): share with one another your key word or phrase and why it has resonated with you.

4. **Prayer** (out loud or in silence): pray, praise, or lament, reflecting on the passage.

5. **Contemplation**: have a moment of silence or listen to or sing 'Psalm 103: Bless the Lord, O my soul' by Kiran Young Wimberly, 'Praise my soul the king of heaven' by Henry Francis Lyte, or '10,000 Reasons' by Matt Redman.

6. **Close**: choose a written prayer (e.g. 1 January) and say it together.

# Notes

1 Kenneth J.Doka (ed.), *Disenfranchised Grief: New directions, challenges, and strategies for practice* (Research Press, 2002).
2 Arlie Russell Hochschild, 'Emotion work, feeling rules, and social structure', *American Journal of Sociology* 85.3 (1979), pp. 551–75, **jstor.org/stable/2778583**
3 Eric Tryggestad, 'Where is God in a war zone?', *The Christian Chronicle*, 1 July 2024, **christianchronicle.org/where-is-god-in-a-war-zone**
4 In conversation with Dr Alfred Sebahene, 5 December 2025.
5 Here, I draw upon Bruce Malina's classics and Zeba Crook's more recent writings on first-century mediterranean cultures.
6 For the full story, read Sheridan Voysey's engaging memoir, *Resurrection Year: Turning broken dreams into new beginnings* (Thomas Nelson, 2013).
7 Sheridan and Merryn Voysey, 'A journey through broken dreams – infertility and childlessness' (video). Our Daily Bread Ministries YouTube Channel, 27 June 2020, **youtu.be/Gd526nRrFm4**
8 David T. Lamb is also the author of several books.
9 Sue Westwood, '"It's the not being seen that is most tiresome": older women, invisibility and social (in)justice', *Journal of Women & Aging* 35.6 (2023), pp. 557–72, **doi.org/10.1080/08952841.2023.2197658**. Other studies provide a fuller view of how ageism and gender interact, for example: Anna E. Kornadt et al., 'Multiple standards of aging: gender-specific age stereotypes in different life domains', *European Journal of Ageing* 10.4 (2013), pp. 335–44, **pmc.ncbi.nlm.nih.gov/articles/PMC5549213**; Laurie Russell Hatch, 'Gender and ageism', *Generations: Journal of the American Society on Aging* 29.3 (2005), pp. 19–24, **jstor.org/stable/26555400**.
10 See further Bruce Malina's writings, though some of his conclusions about shame and being female have been helpfully challenged.
11 Michael Smith, 'Phyllis Latour obituary', *The Guardian*, 13 October 2023, **theguardian.com/world/2023/oct/13/phyllis-latour-obituary**.
12 I do accept, however, that John the Baptist *in utero* may have pipped her to the post.
13 In conversation, December 2025.

**14** Quotes from all three people are from my interviews with them, November and December 2025.

**15** In conversation with Dr Sheila Akomiah-Conteh, 21 November 2025.

**16** This may be because *kataluma* is the 'upper room' that Jesus reserves for the last supper (Luke 22:11). The more common word for 'inn' is *pandocheion* – for example, where the good Samaritan paid for the traveller's lodgings (Luke 10:34).

**17** For example, Kenneth E. Bailey, 'The manger and the inn: the cultural background of Luke 2:7', *Theological Review* 2.2 (1979), pp. 33–44.

**18** Justin Martyr, 'Dialogue with Trypho', *New Advent*, edited by Alexander Roberts, James Donaldson, and A. Cleveland Coxe, translated by Marcus Dods and George Reith, Christian Literature Publishing Co., 1885, **newadvent.org/fathers/0128.htm**, chapter 78.

**19** Michael Green, *The Message of Matthew* (IVP, 2000), p. 68.

**20** Abby Norman, 'Hope is about telling the truth', Sermons and Spirits Substack, 11 December 2025, **abbynormansays.substack.com/p/hope-is-about-telling-the-truth**

**21** Josephus, *Antiquities*, xiv. 15.2.

**22** Open Doors UK and Ireland YouTube channel. 'Millions of Christians are displaced across sub-Saharan Africa– why is no one talking about it?', 27 August 2024, **youtu.be/Wu3Qqzdfac0**

**23** Georgie Tennant, 'Remembering Grace', Some Poems by Georgie blog, 23 December 2014, **somepoemsbygeorgie.blogspot.com/2014/12/remembering-grace.html**. Georgie is the author of *The God Who Sees You: 30 inspiring reflections* (Kevin Mayhew, 2023).

**24** Frederick Buechner, 'Grace', from FrederickBuechner.com, 9 September 2016, **frederickbuechner.com/quote-of-the-day/2016/9/9/grace**.

**25** Steve Legg and Carl Beech, 'SPECIAL: Two evangelists on terminal illness, joy in suffering and praying for healing', Premier Plus Podcast, 26 January 2024, **premier.plus/the-profile/podcasts/episodes/special-two-evangelists-on-terminal-illness-joy-in-suffering-and-praying-for-healing**. See also Steve Legg, *The Last Laugh: Reflections of a funnyman with terminal cancer* (Son Christian Media, 2023).